ISLAM HONORS THE WOMAN

SHAYKH ABDUR RAZZAAQ BIN ABDUL MUHSIN
AL-BADR

@ Maktabatulirshad Publications Ltd, USA

Softcover ISBN: 978-1-9432-8160-2

First Edition : Shawwāl 1436 A.H. / July 2015 C.E.

Cover Design : Maktabatulirshad staff

Translation : Abū Sulaymān Muḥammad ʿAbdul ʿAẓīm

Revision : ʿAbdullāh as-Somalī

Editing : Maktabatulirshad Staff

Typesetting : Abū Sulaymān Muḥammad ʿAbdul-Azīm

Bin Joshua Baker

Subject : Social Issues, Women

Website : www.maktabatulirshad.com

Email : info@maktabatulirshad.com

مكتبة الإرشاد
Maktabatul-Irshad
PUBLICATIONS

Table of Contents

.

BRIEF BIOGRAPHY OF THE AUTHOR

His name: is Shaykh ʿAbdur-Razzāq Ibn ʿAbdul-Muhsin al-ʿAbbād al-Badr, who is the son of the *Allāmah* & *Muhaddith* of *Madinah*, Shaykh ʿAbdul-Muhsin al-ʿAbbād al-Badr.

Birth: He was born on the 22nd day of *Dhul-Qaʾdah* in 1382 A.H. in *az-Zalʾfi*, Kingdom of Saudi Arabia. He currently resides in *Madinah*.

Current Occupation: He is a member of the teaching staff at the Islāmic University of *Madinah*.

Scholarly Certifications: Doctorate in ʿAqīdah.

The Shaykh has authored books, papers of research, as well as numerous explanations in different disciplines. Among them are:

1. *Fiqh of Supplications & Legislative Remembrance.*
2. *Hajj & Refinement of Souls*
3. Explanation of the book, *Exemplary Principles'* by Shaykh Muḥammad ibn Ṣāliḥ al-ʿUthaymīn (رَحِمَهُٱللَّٰه).
4. Explanation of the book, *'the Principles of Names & Attributes'* authored by Shaykh ul-Islām ibn al-Qayyim (رَحِمَهُٱللَّٰه).
5. Explanation of the book, *'Good Words,'* authored by Shaykh ul-Islām ibn al-Qayyim (رَحِمَهُٱللَّٰه).
6. Explanation of the book, *'al-ʿAqīdah Tahaawiyyah.*
7. Explanation of the book, *'al-Fusūl: Biography of the Messenger'* by ibn Kathīr (رَحِمَهُٱللَّٰه).

8. Explanation of the book, 'al-Abab al-Mufrad, by Imām al-Bukhārī (رَحِمَهُ ٱللَّهُ).

He studied knowledge under several scholars. The most distinguished of them are:

1. His father the *Allāmah* Shaykh ʿAbdul-Muhsin al-ʿAbbād al-Badr (حَظِفَهُ اللَّهُ).

2. The *Allāmah* Shaykh ʿAbdul-Azeez bin ʿAbdullāh bin Bāz (رَحِمَهُ ٱللَّهُ).

3. The *Allāmah* Shaykh Muḥammad ibn Ṣāliḥ al-ʿUthaymīn (رَحِمَهُ ٱللَّهُ).

Shaykh ʿAli ibn Nāsir al-Faqīhī (حَظِفَهُ اللَّهُ).

TRANSLITERATION TABLE

Consonants

ء	'	د	d	ض	ḍ	ك	k
ب	b	ذ	dh	ط	ṭ	ل	l
ت	t	ر	r	ظ	ẓ	م	m
ث	th	ز	z	ع	'	ن	n
ج	j	س	s	غ	gh	هـ	h
ح	ḥ	ش	sh	ف	f	و	w
خ	kh	ص	ṣ	ق	q	ي	y

Vowels

Short	´	a	ِ	i	ُ	u
Long	ـَا	ā	ـِي	ī	ـُو	ū

Diphthongs	ـَو	aw	ـَي	ay	

Arabic Symbols & their meanings

عَزَّوَجَلَّ

(Allāh) the
Mighty &
Sublime

سُبْحَانَهُوَتَعَالَى

Glorified &
Exalted is
Allāh

رَحِمَهُٱللَّهُ

May Allāh
have mercy
on him

حَفِظَهُ اللهُ

May Allāh
preserve him

صَلَّىٱللَّهُعَلَيْهِوَعَلَىٰآلِهِوَسَلَّمَ

May Allāh
elevate his rank
& grant him
peace

جَلَّجَلَالُهُ

(Allāh) His
Majesty is
Exalted

جَلَّوَعَلَا

(Allāh) the
Sublime &
Exalted

تَبَارَكَوَتَعَالَى

(Allāh) the
Blessed &
Exalted

رَضِيَٱللَّهُعَنْهُمْ

May Allāh be
pleased with
them

رَضِيَٱللَّهُعَنْهَا

May Allāh be
pleased with
her

رَضِيَٱللَّهُعَنْهُ

May Allāh
be pleased
with him

عَلَيْهِٱلصَّلَاةُوَٱلسَّلَامُ

May Allāh
elevate his rank
& grant him
peace

رَحِمَهُمُٱللَّهُ

May Allāh
have mercy
upon them

INTRODUCTION

All praise belongs to Allāh who perfected our religion and completed His favor upon us; He who has made our nation—the Ummah of Islām—the best nation; He who brought forward a Messenger from amongst us who recited Allāh's verses to us, purified us and taught us the Book and Sunnah. May Allāh send His *Salah* and *Salaam* upon the one who was sent as a mercy to all of mankind; the one who is an example for those who initiate good deeds; and he who is a path for those who tread thereupon. May Allāh's *Salah* and *Salaam* be upon His Messenger, his family, and all of his companions.

To proceed:

Indeed, Allāh's blessing upon His Muslim servant is tremendous, and His kindness to him is enormous as he guided him to this great religion, the religion of Islām—the religion with which Allāh is pleased and completed for His servants. And any religion besides Islām will not be accepted as Allāh (سُبْحَانَهُوَتَعَالَى) says:

$$ ﴿ ٱلْيَوْمَ أَكْمَلْتُ لَكُمْ دِينَكُمْ وَأَتْمَمْتُ عَلَيْكُمْ نِعْمَتِي وَرَضِيتُ لَكُمُ ٱلْإِسْلَٰمَ دِينًا ﴾ $$

"This day, I have perfected your religion for you, completed My Favor upon you, and have chosen

for you Islām as your religion." [Sūrah Al-Māʾidah (5):3]

Allāh (سُبْحَانَهُوَتَعَالَى) also says:

﴿ إِنَّ ٱلدِّينَ عِندَ ٱللَّهِ ٱلْإِسْلَمُ ﴾

"Truly, the religion with Allāh is Islām." [Sūrah ʾĀl-ʿImrān (3):19]

Allāh (سُبْحَانَهُوَتَعَالَى) also says:

﴿ وَمَن يَبْتَغِ غَيْرَ ٱلْإِسْلَمِ دِينًا فَلَن يُقْبَلَ مِنْهُ وَهُوَ فِي ٱلْآخِرَةِ مِنَ ٱلْخَسِرِينَ ۝ ﴾

"And whoever seeks a religion other than Islām, it will never be accepted of him, and in the Hereafter he will be one of the losers." [Sūrah ʾĀl-ʿImrān (3):85]

Allāh (سُبْحَانَهُوَتَعَالَى) also says:

﴿ وَلَكِنَّ ٱللَّهَ حَبَّبَ إِلَيْكُمُ ٱلْإِيمَنَ وَزَيَّنَهُ فِي قُلُوبِكُمْ وَكَرَّهَ إِلَيْكُمُ ٱلْكُفْرَ وَٱلْفُسُوقَ وَٱلْعِصْيَانَ أُوْلَئِكَ هُمُ ٱلرَّاشِدُونَ ۝ فَضْلًا مِّنَ ٱللَّهِ وَنِعْمَةً وَٱللَّهُ عَلِيمٌ حَكِيمٌ ۝ ﴾

"But Allāh has endeared the Faith to you and has beautified it in your hearts, and has made disbelief, wickedness and disobedience (to Allāh and His Messenger) hateful to you. These! They are the rightly guided ones, (This is) a Grace from Allāh and His Favor. And Allāh is All-Knowing, All-Wise." [Sūrah al-Hujurāt (49):7-8]

Indeed, it (Islām) is the religion through which Allāh corrected beliefs, morals and the life of this world as well as the hereafter. Through Islām, Allāh beautifies the external and interior (appearance) of the person. Anyone who embraces and clings to Islām will be liberated from the claws of falsehood, the abyss of turpitude, and the slipperiness of corruption and misguidance.

Indeed, Islām is the correct religion. Its goals, purposes, guidance, directives, results, and benefits have been perfected. Islām's narratives are entirely genuine and sincere. Its rulings are balanced and healthy. Therefore, the legislation will never command a matter and the sound intellect[1] will say, 'I wish Allāh had prohibited it'; and never will the legislation prohibit a matter and the sound intellect will say, 'I wish Allāh had commanded this'; and never will the legislation make a matter lawful and the sound intellect will say, 'I wish Allāh had made it unlawful'; and never will

---

[1] **TN:** what the term 'sound intellect' refers to is the intellect that agrees with the legislation of Allāh that is upon the Fitrah (i.e., natural disposition).

the legislation make a matter unlawful and the sound intellect will say, 'I wish Allāh had made it lawful.'[2]

No correct knowledge had come before disproving any matter of His tremendous narratives, nor had there came a single sound command voiding any of Islām's correct rulings.

Indeed, Islām is the great religion which guides to the truth and an upright path. Truthfulness is Islām's slogan and Justice is its axis. The truth is its makeup, Mercy is its essence and objective, good is its partner, integrity and reform are its beauty and actions, while Guidance and the right path are its provision. For this reason, the greatest form of honor achieved by the servant is guidance to this religion: the success to cling to it, adherence to its guidance, faithfulness to its evidences and directives; and complete remoteness and warning from every forbidden matter.

The honor with which Islām bestows the Muslim woman with is among its perfection and beauty, it is a protection for them. Islām has concern for women's rights and prevents them from being oppressed and transgressed upon, and their

---

[2] **Translator's note:** the author (i.e., Shaykh Abdur Razzaaq ibn Abdul Muhsin al-Badr) may Allāh preserve him, quoted this statement from Ibn Qayyim (May Allāh have mercy upon him) which is in the book *Madaarij Saalikeen* (1/428).

weakness being taken advantage of and what is similar to that.

Islām has made for her and those who live with her tremendous guidelines: instructions filled with wisdom, and upright directives which will ensure for her a pleasant life, an existence full of equality, delight, and happiness in this worldly life and the Hereafter.

ESSENTIAL PRINCIPLES

Regarding this great station, it is imperative for the Muslim to be aware, in summary, of these important principles and great guidelines in order to ascertain knowledge and realization of it (i.e. principles & guidelines) and make advancements according to it. And to similarly learn real commendation, perfect bestowal of favors, and eternal happiness in this worldly life and the Hereafter.

Firstly, the servant should know with complete certainty that the best, most upright, perfect and beautiful rulings are the decrees of the Lord and Creator of all that exists. Allāh (سُبْحَانَهُۥوَتَعَالَىٰ) says:

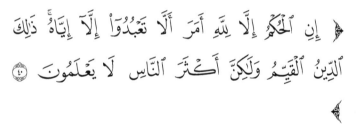

"**The command (or the judgment) is for none but Allāh. He has commanded that you worship none but Him (i.e., His Monotheism), that is the (true) straight religion, but most men know not.**" [Sūrah Yūsuf (12):40]

Allāh (سُبْحَانَهُۥوَتَعَالَىٰ) also says:

﴿ وَمَنْ أَحْسَنُ مِنَ ٱللَّهِ حُكْمًا لِّقَوْمٍ يُوقِنُونَ ۝ ﴾

"And who is better in judgment than Allāh for a people who have firm Faith." [Sūrah Al-Mā'idah (5):50]

Allāh (سُبْحَانَهُوَتَعَالَ) also says:

﴿ وَهُوَ خَيْرُ ٱلْحَاكِمِينَ ۝ ﴾

"And He is the Best of judges." [Sūrah Yūnus (10):109]

Allāh (سُبْحَانَهُوَتَعَالَ) also says:

﴿ أَلَيْسَ ٱللَّهُ بِأَحْكَمِ ٱلْحَاكِمِينَ ۝ ﴾

"Is not Allāh the Best of judges?" [Sūrah at-Tīn 95:8]

Allāh (سُبْحَانَهُوَتَعَالَ) also says:

﴿ كَذَٰلِكَ يُبَيِّنُ ٱللَّهُ لَكُمْ ءَايَٰتِهِۦ وَٱللَّهُ عَلِيمٌ حَكِيمٌ ۝ ﴾

"Thus Allāh makes clear His *Ayat* (Commandments and legal obligations) for you. And Allāh is All-Knowing, All-Wise." [Sūrah an-Nūr (24):59]

Secondly, the servant must understand that his happiness and honor is entirely tied to his obedience to his Lord as well as his abidance to His rulings: his portion and allotment from it is according to his portion and allotment of obedience and abidance. Allāh (سُبْحَانَهُوَتَعَالَى) says:

﴿ إِن تَجْتَنِبُوا۟ كَبَآئِرَ مَا تُنْهَوْنَ عَنْهُ نُكَفِّرْ عَنكُمْ سَيِّـَٔاتِكُمْ وَنُدْخِلْكُم مُّدْخَلًا كَرِيمًا ۝ ﴾

"If you avoid the great sins that you are forbidden to do, We shall remit your (small) sins, and admit you to a Noble Entrance (i.e. Paradise)." [Sūrah An-Nisā' (4):31]

Allāh (سُبْحَانَهُوَتَعَالَى) says about the comrade of Yasin:

﴿ إِنِّىٓ ءَامَنتُ بِرَبِّكُمْ فَٱسْمَعُونِ ۝ قِيلَ ٱدْخُلِ ٱلْجَنَّةَ قَالَ يَٰلَيْتَ قَوْمِى يَعْلَمُونَ ۝ بِمَا غَفَرَ لِى رَبِّى وَجَعَلَنِى مِنَ ٱلْمُكْرَمِينَ ۝ ﴾

"Verily! I have believed in your Lord, so listen to me! It was said (to him when the disbelievers killed him): 'Enter Paradise.' He said: Would that my people knew! That my Lord (Allāh) has forgiven me and made me of the honored ones!" [Yāsīn (36):25-27]

Allāh (سُبْحَانَهُوَتَعَالَى) also says:

$$ \text{﴾ قَدْ أَفْلَحَ مَن زَكَّىٰهَا ۝ وَقَدْ خَابَ مَن دَسَّىٰهَا ۝ ﴿} $$

"Indeed he succeeds who purifies his oneself (i.e., obeys and performs all that Allāh ordered, by following the true Faith of Islāmic Monotheism and by doing righteous good deeds). And indeed he fails who corrupts his ownself." [Sūrah ash-Shams (91):9-10]

Thirdly, the Muslim servant—male or female—should be aware that they have numerous enemies in this worldly life. These enemies are making every effort to topple their dignity, rarefying the path to their might and happiness. They (their enemies) sent forth whatever they are able do to in order to disparage and humiliate them.

At the forefront of these enemies is Shaytaan, the enemy of Allāh, Islām, and His believing servants; he who is infuriated with an extreme level of lividness at Allāh honoring the believers with this religion and guiding them to His straight path. So Shaytaan has declared a large scale war against them and waylays for them at every path He then approaches them from every direction wanting to thwart them from their dignity and trying to cause them to lose their might and prestige. Allāh (سُبْحَانَهُ وَتَعَالَى) says:

$$ \text{﴾ وَإِذْ قُلْنَا لِلْمَلَٰئِكَةِ اسْجُدُوا لِآدَمَ فَسَجَدُوا إِلَّا إِبْلِيسَ قَالَ ءَأَسْجُدُ لِمَنْ خَلَقْتَ طِينًا ۝ قَالَ ﴿} $$

أَرَءَيْتَكَ هَٰذَا ٱلَّذِى كَرَّمْتَ عَلَىَّ لَئِنْ أَخَّرْتَنِ إِلَىٰ يَوْمِ ٱلْقِيَٰمَةِ لَأَحْتَنِكَنَّ ذُرِّيَّتَهُۥٓ إِلَّا قَلِيلًا ۞ قَالَ ٱذْهَبْ فَمَن تَبِعَكَ مِنْهُمْ فَإِنَّ جَهَنَّمَ جَزَآؤُكُمْ جَزَآءً مَّوْفُورًا ۞ وَٱسْتَفْزِزْ مَنِ ٱسْتَطَعْتَ مِنْهُم بِصَوْتِكَ وَأَجْلِبْ عَلَيْهِم بِخَيْلِكَ وَرَجِلِكَ وَشَارِكْهُمْ فِى ٱلْأَمْوَٰلِ وَٱلْأَوْلَٰدِ وَعِدْهُمْ وَمَا يَعِدُهُمُ ٱلشَّيْطَٰنُ إِلَّا غُرُورًا ۞

"And (remember) when We said to the angels: "Prostrate unto Adam." They prostrated except *Iblîs* (Satan). He said: "Shall I prostrate to one whom You created from clay?" [*Iblîs* (Satan)] said: "See? This one whom You have honored above me, if You give me respite (keep me alive) to the Day of Resurrection, I will surely seize and mislead his offspring (by sending them astray) all but a few!" (Allāh) said: "Go, and whosoever of them follows you, surely! Hell will be the recompense of you (all) an ample recompense. "And *Istafziz* [literally means: befool them gradually] those whom you can among them with your voice (i.e. songs, music, and any other call for Allāh's disobedience), make assaults on them with your cavalry and your infantry, mutually share with them wealth and children (by tempting them to earn money by illegal ways usury, etc., or by committing illegal sexual intercourse, etc.), and make promises to them." But Satan promises them nothing but deceit." [Sūrah Al-ʾIsrāʾ (17):61-64]

And Allāh (سُبْحَانَهُوَتَعَالَى) says:

$$﴾ إِنَّ ٱلشَّيْطَٰنَ لَكُمْ عَدُوٌّ فَٱتَّخِذُوهُ عَدُوًّا ۚ إِنَّمَا يَدْعُواْ$$

$$حِزْبَهُۥ لِيَكُونُواْ مِنْ أَصْحَٰبِ ٱلسَّعِيرِ ۝ ﴿$$

"Surely, *Shaytaan* is an enemy to you, so take (treat) him as an enemy. He only invites his *Hizb* (followers) that they may become the dwellers of the blazing Fire." [Sūrah Fāṭir (35):6]

Hence, it is incumbent upon every Muslim, male and female, to be cautious of Shaytaan and every enemy that aims to dislodge them both from this station of honor.

<u>Fourthly</u>, one must believe his success, probity of his affairs, straightness of his condition, and ascertainment of his honor is in his Master and Lord's hand. The Lord of Might (سُبْحَانَهُوَتَعَالَى) says:

$$﴾ وَمَن يُهِنِ ٱللَّهُ فَمَا لَهُۥ مِن مُّكْرِمٍ ۚ إِنَّ ٱللَّهَ$$

$$يَفْعَلُ مَا يَشَآءُ ۩ ۝ ﴿$$

"And whomsoever Allāh disgraces, none can honor him. Verily! Allāh does what He wills." [Sūrah al-Ḥajj (22):18]

For this reason, it is incumbent upon him to strengthen his bond with His Lord (سُبْحَانَهُوَتَعَالَى) and he seek his honor from Him. From the supplications of the Prophet (صَلَّ ٱللَّهُ عَلَيْهِ وَسَلَّمَ) is:

اللَّهُمَّ أَصْلِحْ لِي دِينِي الَّذِي هُوَ عِصْمَةُ أَمْرِي، وَأَصْلِحْ لِي دُنْيَايَ الَّتِي فِيهَا مَعَاشِي، وَ أَصْلِحْ لِي آخِرَتِي الَّتِي فِيهَا مَعَادِي، وَاجْعَلِ الْحَيَاةَ زِيَادَةً لِي فِي كُلِّ خَيْرٍ، وَ الْمَوْتَ رَاحَةً لِي مِنْ كُلِّ شَرٍّ.

"O Allāh, make my religion easy for me by virtue of which my affairs are protected; set right for me my world where my life exists, make good for me my Hereafter which is my resort to which I have to return and make my life prone to perform all types of good, and make death a comfort for me from every evil." [3]

This statement serves to indicate that no one can do without His Lord granting uprightness of his situations, straightness

---

[3] *Muslim* reported it (272).

of his affairs, and ascertainment of his dignity and conferment of honors.

Fifthly, he must make his greatest concern in this worldly life to be honored before Allāh, so he can obtain conferment of honors and become happy with what Allāh (سُبْحَانَهُوَتَعَالَى) has prepared for His honored servants whom Allāh says regarding them:

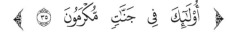

"Such shall dwell in the Gardens (i.e. Paradise) honored." [Sūrah al-Mʿirāj (70):35]

So this is a true honor and the only way to achieve this is by carrying out the Taqwā of Allāh (سُبْحَانَهُوَتَعَالَى) in secret and in open, and in the witnessed and unseen. Allāh (سُبْحَانَهُوَتَعَالَى) says,

﴿ إِنَّ أَكْرَمَكُمْ عِندَ ٱللَّهِ أَتْقَىٰكُمْ ﴾

"Verily, the most honorable of you with Allāh is that (believer) who has *at-Taqwa*." [*Soorah al-Hujuraat* 49:13]

In Ṣaḥīḥ Bukhārī on the authority of Abū Hurairah (رَضِيَٱللَّهُعَنْهُ) who said:

قِيـلَ لِـلـنَّـبِـيِّ صَـلَّـى اللهُ عَـلَـيْـهِ وَ سَـلَّـمَ : مَـنْ
أَكْـرَمُ الـنَّـاسِ؟ قَـالَ : ((أَكْـرَمُـهُـمْ أَتْـقَـاهُـمْ)) .

"The Prophet (ﷺ) was asked, 'Who is the most honorable of the people?' He said, 'the most distinguished of them with Allāh are those who have Taqwā.'" [4]

Whoever seeks honor from other than this way, then he will only be chasing after a mirage and pursuing a path of failure and ruin.

Sixthly, the woman specifically must know that the rulings related to her affairs are at the utmost perfection and mastery without even a single flaw or imperfection, nor any bias or offense. And why would it not be so when these are the judgments of the best of Judges, the revelation of the Lord of all that exists: *al-Hakeem* (i.e. The All-Wise) in His administration (of His creation), *al-Baseer* (i.e. The All-Seeing) of His servants, *al-'Aleem* (i.e. The All-Knowing) of what is their happiness, success, and righteousness in this world and the hereafter.

For this reason, from the greatest oppression and most severe crime and abasement is that one says regarding anything from Allāh's rulings related to the woman or other than her,

---

[4] *Al-Bukhārī* collected it (3374).

"Indeed within them (i.e., the judgments) is bias, deprivation, injustice, or offense." And the one who makes these statements or some of them has not estimated his Lord with an estimation due to Him, nor has he respected Him. Allāh (عَزَّوَجَلَّ) says:

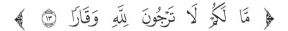

"What is the matter with you, [that you fear not Allāh (His punishment), and] you hope not for reward." [Sūrah Nūḥ (71):13]

Meaning, what is the matter with you that you do not treat Him like those who respect Him. The word **'respect'** refers to veneration, and from veneration of Him (سُبْحَانَهُوَتَعَالَ) is that His judgments are upheld and His commands obeyed. It is believed that within these judgments is integrity, superiority, and prestige; and whoever believes contrary to that then how remote is he from venerating [Allāh] and how befitting is he to be humiliated and shamed in this world and the Hereafter.

So it is proper to be conscious of these essential principles and great guidelines and to give them great concern regarding this subject; rather, they are in reality thereinforcementswhich these principles and guidelines are built upon and the foundations that they are established on.

WHO IS THE WOMAN?

The word *"al-mara'tu"* (woman) in the Arabic language refers to the female version of the male. Its pronunciation is *"imra'tun"* or *"mar'ah"* and it does not have a plural form (in Arabic); the word *nisā'* or *niswah* is instead used. The woman is the creation that Allāh (عَزَّوَجَلَّ) has brought into existence as a partner for man throughout his life. She was created originally from man in order for the similitude to be more profound and the bond and nearness to one another more Ibnding; and also so that the sincere affection and mercy between them can be actualized in the most splendid fashion and beautiful appearance. Allāh (سُبْحَانَهُۥوَتَعَالَى) says:

﴿ يَٰٓأَيُّهَا ٱلنَّاسُ ٱتَّقُواْ رَبَّكُمُ ٱلَّذِى خَلَقَكُم مِّن نَّفۡسٍ وَٰحِدَةٍ وَخَلَقَ مِنۡهَا زَوۡجَهَا وَبَثَّ مِنۡهُمَا رِجَالًا كَثِيرًا وَنِسَآءً وَٱتَّقُواْ ٱللَّهَ ٱلَّذِى تَسَآءَلُونَ بِهِۦ وَٱلۡأَرۡحَامَ إِنَّ ٱللَّهَ كَانَ عَلَيۡكُمۡ رَقِيبًا ١ ﴾

"O mankind! Be dutiful to your Lord, Who created you from a single person (Adam), and from him (Adam) He created his wife [Hawwaa' (Eve)], and from them both He created many men and women and fear Allāh through Whom you demand your mutual (rights), and (do not cut the relations of) the wombs (kinship). Surely, Allāh is Ever an All-Watcher over you." [Sūrah An-Nisā' (4):1]

He (سُبْحَانَهُوَتَعَالَى) also says:

﴿ وَمِنْ ءَايَتِهِۦٓ أَنْ خَلَقَ لَكُم مِّنْ أَنفُسِكُمْ أَزْوَٰجًا لِّتَسْكُنُوٓاْ إِلَيْهَا وَجَعَلَ بَيْنَكُم مَّوَدَّةً وَرَحْمَةً إِنَّ فِى ذَٰلِكَ لَأَيَٰتٍ لِّقَوْمٍ يَتَفَكَّرُونَ ﴾ ۝

"And among His Signs is this, that He created for you wives from among yourselves, that you may find repose in them, and He has put between you affection and mercy. Verily, in that are indeed signs for a people who reflect." [Sūrah Al-Rūm (30):21]

He (سُبْحَانَهُوَتَعَالَى) also says:

﴿ وَٱللَّهُ جَعَلَ لَكُم مِّنْ أَنفُسِكُمْ أَزْوَٰجًا وَجَعَلَ لَكُم مِّنْ أَزْوَٰجِكُم بَنِينَ وَحَفَدَةً وَرَزَقَكُم مِّنَ ٱلطَّيِّبَٰتِ أَفَبِٱلْبَٰطِلِ يُؤْمِنُونَ وَبِنِعْمَتِ ٱللَّهِ هُمْ يَكْفُرُونَ ﴾ ۝

"And Allāh has made for you wives of your kind, and has made for you, from your wives, sons and grandsons, and has bestowed on you good provision. Do they then believe in false deities and deny the Favour of Allāh (by not worshipping Allāh Alone)." [Sūrah Al-Naḥl (16):72]

These verses bespeak that Hawwaa', the wife of Aadam (عَلَيْهِالسَّلَامُ), was created from him; then Allāh (سُبْحَانَهُوَتَعَالَى) spread from them countless men and women through their copulation which resulted in pregnancy and procreation.

Allāh made for the man components and characteristics, just as He similarly created for the woman her components and characteristics; thus their divergence from their respected components and characteristics is deemed a deviation from the natural disposition [that each was created upon] and a departure from the path. It has been confirmed in *Bukhārī* and *Muslim* from the Ḥadīth of Abū Hurairah (رَضِيَاللَّهُعَنْهُ) that the Prophet (صَلَّىاللَّهُعَلَيْهِوَسَلَّمَ) said:

إِنَّ الْمَرْأَةَ خُلِقَتْ مِنْ ضِلَعٍ ، وَ إِنَّ أَعْوَجَ شَيْءٍ فِي الضِّلَعِ أَعْلَاهُ ، فَإِنْ ذَهَبْتَ تُقِيمُهُ كَسَرْتَهُ ، وَ إِنِ اسْتَمْتَعْتَ بِهَا اسْتَمْتَعْتَ بِهَا وَ فِيهَا عِوَجٌ .

"Indeed the woman was created from a rib, and its most crooked part is the uppermost. If you attempt to straighten it; you will break it, and if you enjoy her, you will do so while crookedness remains in her." [5]

---

[5] *Al-Bukhārī* (3331) and *Muslim* collected it (1468).

an-Nawawee (رَحِمَهُ ٱللَّهُ) commented on this Ḥadīth saying,

"Within this Ḥadīth is a proof to what the scholars of Fiqh or some of them state that Hawwaa' was created from the rib of Aadam. Allāh (سُبْحَانَهُ وَتَعَالَى) says, 'Who created you from a single person (Aadam), and from him (Aadam) He created his wife [Hawwaa' (Eve)].'" [6]

This statement denotes that the core of the woman's structure and natural disposition has been made distinct with some characteristics and components which cause her to have a particular state and individual style of life which begins with her femininity, motherhood, gentleness, vulnerability, and abundant mood swings. So she menstruates, becomes pregnant, has cravings for particular food while pregnant, gives birth, breastfeeds, concerns herself with the nurturing of her newborn and other than that from what she specializes in. And just like this the man has components and characteristics of his own; neither side should aspire for the other's characteristics as Allāh (سُبْحَانَهُ وَتَعَالَى) says:

﴿ وَلَا تَتَمَنَّوْاْ مَا فَضَّلَ ٱللَّهُ بِهِۦ بَعْضَكُمْ عَلَىٰ بَعْضٍ لِّلرِّجَالِ نَصِيبٌ مِّمَّا ٱكْتَسَبُواْ وَلِلنِّسَآءِ نَصِيبٌ ﴾

---

[6] Explanation of *Ṣaḥīḥ Muslim* (10/57).

مِّمَّا ٱكْتَسَبْنَ وَسْئَلُوا۟ ٱللَّهَ مِن فَضْلِهِۦٓ إِنَّ ٱللَّهَ كَانَ بِكُلِّ شَىْءٍ عَلِيمًا ۞ ﴾

"And wish not for the things in which Allāh has made some of you to excel others. For men, there is a reward for what they have earned, (and likewise) for women there is a reward for what they have earned, and ask Allāh of His Bounty. Surely, Allāh is Ever All-Knower of everything." [Sūrah An-Nisā' (4):32]

And He (سُبْحَانَهُوَتَعَالَى) says:

﴿ ٱلرِّجَالُ قَوَّٰمُونَ عَلَى ٱلنِّسَآءِ بِمَا فَضَّلَ ٱللَّهُ بَعْضَهُمْ عَلَىٰ بَعْضٍ وَبِمَآ أَنفَقُوا۟ مِنْ أَمْوَٰلِهِمْ ﴾

"Men are the protectors and maintainers of women, because Allāh has made one of them to excel the other, and because they spend (to support them) from their means." [Sūrah An-Nisā' (4):34]

The man's custodianship over the woman is from the things that Allāh has made whereby one of them excels over the other. From these matters with which man has been made particular with is superiority in intellect, sedateness, patience, perseverance, self-control, and strength which the woman does not have the likeness thereof. Thus the man has been given certain rights over the woman that are in harmony with her abilities and the core of her makeup, and likewise the woman has been given individual rights over the man that are in harmony with his abilities and the core of his makeup.

WHAT IS THE REALITY CONCERNING HONOR GIVEN TO MAN?

One who contemplates over the texts and evidences will find that Allāh's bestowing of honor on man is of two types:

A general honor: Allāh (سُبْحَانَهُوَتَعَالَى) clarifies this with His statement,

﴿ ۞ وَلَقَدْ كَرَّمْنَا بَنِىٓ ءَادَمَ وَحَمَلْنَٰهُمْ فِى ٱلْبَرِّ وَٱلْبَحْرِ وَرَزَقْنَٰهُم مِّنَ ٱلطَّيِّبَٰتِ وَفَضَّلْنَٰهُمْ عَلَىٰ كَثِيرٍ مِّمَّنْ خَلَقْنَا تَفْضِيلًا ۞ ﴾

"And indeed We have honored the Children of Aadam, and We have carried them on land and sea, and have provided them with *at-Taiyibât* (lawful good things), and have preferred them above many of those whom We have created with a marked preference." [Sūrah Al-'Isrā' (17):70]

al-Qurtubi (رَحِمَهُ ٱللَّهُ) said about this verse:

"This honor includes their creation in this certain appearance which is of a wide figure and a beautiful shape; and their being carried through land and sea—a privilege which is not achieved by

any creature accept the children of Aadam. So by His supreme will, design, governing, and His honoring man Allāh takes upon Himself bestows upon man their allotment of food, drink, and clothing; and this is not accommodated for animals like it is for humans. This is the case because they exclusively attain wealth—unlike animals—wear clothes, and eat food prepared from different ingredients whereas the goal of every animal is to simply eat raw meat or food that is not prepared from different ingredients."[7]

And Ibn Kathīr (رَحِمَهُ ٱللَّهُ) said about this verse:

"He (سُبْحَانَهُ وَتَعَالَى) informs us of His gracing the children of Aadam and bestowing honor on them by creating them in the most excellent and perfect appearance just as He (سُبْحَانَهُ وَتَعَالَى) says, ' Verily, We created man of the best stature (mold),' [8] meaning, he walks upright with his two feet and eats with his hands whereas animals walk on all fours and eat with their mouth. Man can differentiate between things and come to know its benefits,

---

[7] From the book, "al-Jaami li Ahkaam-il-Quran" (10/299).

[8] [Soorah at-Teen 95:4]

characteristics and harms in both religious and worldly matters."[9]

An exclusive honor: and this is the guidance to this religion and success towards being obedient to the Lord of all that exists. This is the real honor, the perfect glory, and eternal happiness in this world and the Hereafter since Islām is surely the religion of Allāh (the Mighty and Sublime), the religion of might and honor, loftiness, and uprightness. The might belongs to Allāh, His Messenger and believers.

While clarifying that honor comes only by obedience and submission to His greatness, abidance to His Majesty, and complying with His commands, Allāh (سُبْحَانَهُوَتَعَالَى) says:

$$﴿ أَلَمْ تَرَ أَنَّ ٱللَّهَ يَسْجُدُ لَهُۥ مَن فِى ٱلسَّمَٰوَٰتِ وَمَن$$

$$فِى ٱلْأَرْضِ وَٱلشَّمْسُ وَٱلْقَمَرُ وَٱلنُّجُومُ وَٱلْجِبَالُ وَٱلشَّجَرُ$$

$$وَٱلدَّوَآبُّ وَكَثِيرٌ مِّنَ ٱلنَّاسِ وَكَثِيرٌ حَقَّ عَلَيْهِ ٱلْعَذَابُ وَمَن$$

$$يُهِنِ ٱللَّهُ فَمَا لَهُۥ مِن مُّكْرِمٍ إِنَّ ٱللَّهَ يَفْعَلُ مَا يَشَآءُ$$

$$۝ ﴿١٨﴾ ۝$$

---

[9] From the book, "*Tafseer al-Quran al-'Atheem*" (3/51).

"See you not that to Allāh prostrates whoever is in the heavens and whoever is on the earth, and the sun, and the moon, and the stars, and the mountains, and the trees, and *ad-Dawâb* (moving living creatures, beasts, etc.), and many of mankind? But there are many (men) on whom the punishment is justified. And whomsoever Allāh disgraces, none can honor him. Verily! Allāh does what He wills." [Sūrah al-Ḥajj (22):18]

So the one who has not been granted success to having ʾĪmān (i.e., true Islāmic faith) and does not abide by the obedience of the Most Gracious, then he is humiliated, not honored; and one's portion of honor and safety from humiliation is according to his portion of ʾĪmān in speech, belief, and action. Thus whoever seeks might without the religion will be humiliated and whoever aspires to honor without Islām will be humiliated.

From the things that one must know here is that the bestowement of the first type of honor—which is the general honor—necessitates from man that he fulfill the means to obtain the second type of honor (i.e., the exclusive honor). This means that the one whom Allāh honors with wealth, health, well-being and so forth, must strive to do his utmost in obedience and put forth his efforts for the cause of Allāh's pleasure; because, Allāh (عَزَّوَجَلَّ) will question him on the day of resurrection concerning this honor that he was bestowed.

Imam Muslim collected in his *Ṣaḥīḥ* from the Ḥadīth of Abū
Hurairah (رَضِيَاللَّهُعَنْهُ) that he said:

قَالُـوا يَـا رَسُولَ اللهِ هَـلْ نَـرَى رَبَّنَـا يَـوْمَ الْقِيَامَةِ
؟ قَـالَ : ((هَـلْ تـضَـارُّونَ فِي رُؤْيَـةِ الـشَّمْـسِ فِي
الـظَّـهِـيـرَةِ لَـيْـسَـتْ فِـي سَـحَابَةٍ؟ قَـالُـوا : لَا ،
قَـالَ : فَـهَـلْ تـضَـارُّونَ فِي رُؤْيَـةِ الْقَـمَـرِ لَـيْـلَـةَ
الْـبَـدَرِ لَـيْسَ فِي سَحَابَةٍ ؟ قَالُوا : لَا ، قَالَ :
فَـوَالَّـذِي نَـفْـسِي بِـيَـدِهِ لَا تَـضَارُّونَ فِي رُؤْيَـةِ
رَبِّـكُـمْ إِلَّا كَـمَـا تـضَارُّونَ فِي رُؤْيَـةِ أَحَـدِهِـمَـا ،
قَـالَ : فَـيَـلْـقَـى الْـعَـبْـدُ فَـيَـقُـولُ : أَي فُـلْ أَ لَـمْ
أُكْـرِمْـكَ وَ أُسَـوِّدْكَ وَ أُزَوِّجْـكَ وَ أُسَـخِّـرْ لَـكَ الْـخَـيْـلَ
وَ الْإِبْـلَ وَ أذرك تـرأس وَ تربع ؟ فَـيَـقُـولُ : بَـلَـى ،
قَـالَ : فَـيَـقُـولُ: أَ فَظَـنَـنْتَ أَنَّكَ مُـلَاقِـيّ؟ فَـيَـقُـولُ
: لَا ، فَـيَـقُـولُ : فَـإِنِّي أَنْـسَـاكَ كَـمَـا نَـسِـيتَـنِي ،
ثُـمَّ يَـلْـقَـى الثَّـانِي فَـيَـقُـولُ : أَي فُـلْ أَ لَـمْ ـ لَـمْ
أُكْـرِمْـكَ وَ أُسَـوِّدْكَ وَ أُزَوِّجْـكَ وَ أُسَـخِّـرْ لَـكَ الْـخَـيْـلَ
وَ الْإِبْـلَ وَ أذرك تـرأس وَ تربع ؟ فَـيَـقُـولُ : بَـلَـى

أَي رَبّ ، فَيَقُولُ : أَ فَظَنَنْتَ أَنَّكَ مُلَاقِيّ ؟
فَيَقُولُ : لَا ، فَيَقُولُ : فَإِنِّي أَنْسَاكَ كَمَا
نَسِيتَنِي ، ثُمَّ يَلْقَى الثَّالِثُ فَيَقُولُ لَهُ
مِثْلَ ذَلِكَ فَيَقُولُ : يَا رَبِّ آمَنْتُ بِكَ وَ
بِكِتَابِكَ وَ بِرُسُلِكَ . وَ صَلَّيْتُ وَ صُمْتُ وَ
تَصَدَّقْتُ . وَ يُثْنِي بِخَيْرٍ مَا اسْتَطَاعَ ،
فَيَقُولُ: هَا هُنَا إِذًا ، قَالَ : ثُمَّ يُقَالُ لَهُ : الْآنَ
نَبْعَثُ شَاهِدًا عَلَيْكَ ، وَ يَتَفَكَّرُ فِي نَفْسِهِ
مَنْ ذَا الَّذِي يَشْهَدُ عَلَيَّ ؟! فَيُخْتَمُ عَلَى
فِيهِ وَ يُقَالُ لِفَخِذِهِ وَ لَحْمِهِ وَ عِظَامِهِ
اِنْطِقِي فَتَنْطِقُ فَخِذُهُ وَ لَحْمُهُ وَ عِظَامُهُ
بِعَمَلِهِ ، وَ ذَلِكَ لِيُعذر مِنْ نَفْسِهِ ، وَ ذَلِكَ
الْمُنَافِقُ ، وَ ذَلِكَ الَّذِي يَسْخَطُ اللهُ عَلَيْهِ))
. قَوْلُهُ : ((أَي فُلْ)) أَيْ : يَا فُلَان .

**"They said, 'O Allāh's Messenger, will we be able
to see our Lord on the Day of Judgment? He said:
Do you experience any difficulty in seeing the sun
in the noon when there is no cloud over it? They
said: No. He again said: Do you experience feel any**

difficulty in seeing the moon on the fourteenth night when there is no cloud over it? They said: No. After that he said: By Allāh, Who in His Hand is my life, you will not face any difficulty in seeing your Lord just as you will not do so in seeing one of them. Then Allāh would sit in judgment upon the servant and say: O so and so, did I not honour you and grant you authority, and a spouse and subdue for you horses and camels; as well as afford you an opportunity to rule over your subjects? He would say: Yes. And then Allāh would ask: Did you not think that you would meet me? And he would say: No. After that, He (Allāh) would say: Well, We will forget you as you forgot me. Then the second person would be brought for judgment and Allāh would say: O so and so, did I not honour you and grant you authority, and a spouse and subdue for you horses and camels; as well as afford you an opportunity to rule over your subjects? He would say: Yes, my Lord. And He (the Lord) would say: Did you not think that you would be meeting me? And he would say: No. And then He (Allāh) would say: Well, I will forget you today as you forgot me. Then the third one would be brought, and He (Allāh) would say to him as He said before. And he (the third person) would say: O my Lord, I affirmed my faith in Thee and in Thy Book and in Thy Messenger and I observed prayer and fast and gave charity; and he would speak in good terms like this as much as he is able. And He (Allāh) would say: Well, We will bring our witnesses against you, after which the man would wonder who would bear witness against him. **Then his mouth would be sealed and it would be said to his thighs, flesh and bones to speak; and so his thighs, flesh and bones would bear witness to his deeds and it would be done so that he should not be able to make any excuse for himself, and that is the example of the hypocrite and what Allāh is displeased with.**" [10]

This Ḥadīth is a clear proof that man will be questioned on the day of resurrection concerning how Allāh has honored him with well-being, health, wealth, shelter, food, drink and so forth since Allāh (سُبْحَانَهُوَتَعَالَى) has honored him thus so that he can fulfill His obedience and perform deeds seeking His pleasure. Thus when one directs the blessings unjustly and utilizes it ill-mannerly, he will be held accountable for that on the day of resurrection.

---

[10] Muslim reported it (#2978).

THE WOMAN'S HONOR IN ISLĀM

Indeed, the true religion of Islām with its sound directives and wise directions safeguards the Muslim woman, and protects her integrity and honor. Also, it promises to ensure her high rank and happiness while facilitating for her a pleasant life—one that is distant from areas of skepticism, *fitan*, evil and corruption. All of this is from Allāh's great mercy upon His servants as He sent down His legislation as a sincere advice to them, as a reform for their corruption, as a rectifier of their twistedness and as a guarantee for their happiness.

This great management that Islām has brought for the woman is considered a safety valve for her—rather, for the society as whole with its families—from the release of evil, *fitan,* and the descending of calamities and catastrophes upon them. And if they stray from Islām's guidelines for the woman within society, destruction will be released upon them and evil and danger will come successively. History is the greatest testament to this since whoever reflects on the past with it's extended length will find that the greatest cause for the downfall of civilizations, the dismount of societies, the gradual disappearance of morals, the spread of depravities, the corruption of values, and the outbreak of crimes is the woman improperly beautifying herself, unveiling her face, mingling with men, exaggerating in her beautification, intermingling, being alone with strange men (i.e., those who are unlawful for her to be alone with), and frequenting public forums while she is in a complete state of beautification, most radiant dress, and is well perfumed.

Ibn al-Qayyim (رَحِمَهُ اللّٰهُ) said:

"No doubt that enabling women to intermingle with men is the origin of every calamity and evil. It is amongst the greatest causes for the descent of widespread punishments just as it is amongst the causes of public corruption and exclusive crime. Men mingling with women is a cause for abundant acts of lewdness and fornication, and it is also among the causes of mass deaths and concurrent plagues[11]. When the prostitutes mingled with Musa's army and fornication became widespread amongst them, Allāh sent down upon them a plague and seven thousand people died in one day. This story is well-known in the books of Tafseer. So amongst the greatest causes of massive deaths is the abundance of fornication which is created by enabling women to intermingle with men, and to walk amongst them improperly-covered and beautified. Had the rulers knew what lies in this of corruption for this world and the people, before

---

[11] The Shaykh said commenting on this word, "**like AIDS, syphilis, tuberculosis, and so forth.**"

**considering its graveness in the religion, they would
be the most severe in preventing it.”[12]**

Hence Islām has come with preventive procedures and
curative steps that cut off the root of these *Fitan* and work to
liberate the society from these ills and evils: these are blessed
teachings that aid in avoiding destruction, distancing oneself
from lewdness and ruin—a mercy from Allāh upon the
servants—as well as safegaurding their honor and shielding
them from the humiliation of the worldly life and the
punishment of the Hereafter.

Islām mentions that when the *fitnah* of women occurs, it will
result in corruptions, evils and dangers whose extent is
unknown and whose end dispraised.

Al-Bukhārī and Muslim collected it from the Ḥadīth of Abū
Usaamah Ibn Zayd (رَضِيَٱللَّهُعَنْهُمَا) that the Prophet (صَلَّىٱللَّهُعَلَيْهِوَسَلَّمَ)
said,

$$مَا تَرَكْتُ بَعْدِي فِتْنَةً أَضَرَّ عَلَى الرِّجَالِ مِنَ النِّسَاءِ$$

---

[12] In the book, "*at-Turuq al-Hakamiyyah*" (page 281).

"I have not left after me a greater a *fitnah* (i.e., trial and temptation) more harmful to men than women." [13]

And Muslim collected it in his Ṣaḥīḥ on the authority of Abū Saʿīd al-Khudrī (رَضِيَ ٱللَّهُ عَنْهُ) that the Prophet (صَلَّى ٱللَّهُ عَلَيْهِ وَسَلَّمَ) said:

فَـاتَّـقُـوا الـدُّنْـيَـا وَاتَّـقُـوا الـنِّـسَـاءَ فَـإِنَّ أَوَّلَ فِـتْـنَـةِ بَـنِي إِسْـرَائِـيـلَ كَـانَـتْ فِـي الـنِّـسَـاءِ.

"Be weary of the Dunya (i.e. worldly life), and be weary of Women; for indeed the first *fitnah* of the children of Israel was women." [14]

And because of this, Islām has made for the woman and man from the upright guidelines and significant directives that when established, all the good, virtues, and honor in this world and the hereafter will be actuated. Allāh (سُبْحَانَهُ وَتَعَالَى) says:

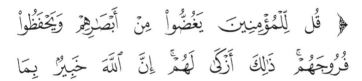

﴿ قُل لِّلْمُؤْمِنِينَ يَغُضُّوا مِنْ أَبْصَارِهِمْ وَيَحْفَظُوا فُرُوجَهُمْ ذَٰلِكَ أَزْكَىٰ لَهُمْ إِنَّ ٱللَّهَ خَبِيرٌ بِمَا

---

[13] al-Bukhārī (5096) and Muslim (2940) collected it.

[14] Muslim collected it (2742).

يَصْنَعُونَ ۞ وَقُل لِّلْمُؤْمِنَٰتِ يَغْضُضْنَ مِنْ
أَبْصَٰرِهِنَّ وَيَحْفَظْنَ فُرُوجَهُنَّ ﴾

"Tell the believing men to lower their gaze (from looking at forbidden things), and protect their private parts (from illegal sexual acts, etc.). That is purer for them. Verily, Allāh is All-Aware of what they do. And tell the believing women to lower their gaze (from looking at forbidden things), and protect their private parts (from illegal sexual acts, etc.)." [Sūrah an-Nūr (24):30-31]

And He (سُبْحَانَهُوَتَعَالَىٰ) says:

﴿ يَٰنِسَآءَ ٱلنَّبِيِّ لَسْتُنَّ كَأَحَدٍ مِّنَ ٱلنِّسَآءِ إِنِ
ٱتَّقَيْتُنَّ فَلَا تَخْضَعْنَ بِٱلْقَوْلِ فَيَطْمَعَ ٱلَّذِى فِى قَلْبِهِۦ
مَرَضٌ وَقُلْنَ قَوْلًا مَّعْرُوفًا ۞ وَقَرْنَ فِى بُيُوتِكُنَّ
وَلَا تَبَرَّجْنَ تَبَرُّجَ ٱلْجَٰهِلِيَّةِ ٱلْأُولَىٰ ﴾

"O wives of the Prophet! You are not like any other women. If you keep your duty (to Allāh), then be not soft in speech, lest he in whose heart is a disease (of hypocrisy, or evil desire for adultery, etc.) should be moved with desire, but speak in an honorable manner. And stay in your houses, and do not display yourselves like that of the times of ignorance." [Sūrah al-ʾAḥzāb (33):32-33]

And He (سُبْحَانَهُوَتَعَالَى) says:

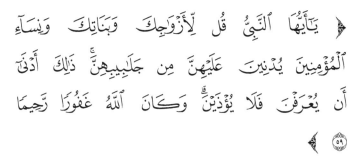

"**O Prophet! Tell your wives and your daughters and the women of the believers to draw their cloaks (veils) all over their bodies (i.e. screen themselves completely except the eyes or one eye to see the way). That will be better, that they should be known (as free respectable women) so as not to be annoyed. And Allāh is Ever Oft-Forgiving, Most Merciful.**" [Sūrah al-ʾAḥzāb (33):59]

The texts concerning this meaning in the Qurʾān and the Sunnah are numerous. And the religion of Islām did not impose these guidelines inorder to suppress liberties, nor for the purpose of constraining people; rather, they are for preserving society, maintaining its virtues, might and honor.

Nor did the religion of Islām impose these guidelines on the Muslim woman inorder to suppress her freedom, rather, Islām came to protect her from indecency, safeguard her from exposure to lewdness, and prevent her from falling into crime and corruption; and to also clothe her with garments of *Taqwā*, purity and modesty. So by that, Islām blocks any excuse that would lead to lewdness and plunge one into depravity—this is the true honor for the woman.

FROM THE QURAN'S GUIDANCE CONCERNING BENEFICENCE TO THE WOMAN

Whoever contemplates over the Book of Allāh (عَزَّوَجَلَّ) that He has revealed to His servants as a guidance, mercy, radiance, light and a reminder for those who remember, will discover within it great consideration for the woman's state and an intense warning against oppressing and violating her.

There are honoroble verses within the Noble Qur'ān that greatly resolve this matter: there is Sūrah an-Nisā' which contains numerous verses associated with women and a clarification of their tremendous rights. Among the Qur'ān's guidance concerning kindness to women are the following:

First: The command to deal with the woman within the limits of what is good religiously and beneficence: a conforming to great boundaries and straight guidelines. Also, it warns from oppressing her or violating Allāh's boundaries which He has legislated for His servants in dealing with her. Allāh (سُبْحَانَهُوَتَعَالَى) says:

﴿ ٱلطَّلَٰقُ مَرَّتَانِۖ فَإِمْسَاكٌ بِمَعْرُوفٍ أَوْ تَسْرِيحٌ بِإِحْسَٰنٍۗ وَلَا يَحِلُّ لَكُمْ أَن تَأْخُذُواْ مِمَّآ ءَاتَيْتُمُوهُنَّ شَيْئًا إِلَّآ أَن يَخَافَآ أَلَّا يُقِيمَا حُدُودَ ٱللَّهِۖ فَإِنْ خِفْتُمْ أَلَّا

يُقِيمَا حُدُودَ ٱللَّهِ فَلَا جُنَاحَ عَلَيْهِمَا فِيمَا ٱفْتَدَتْ بِهِۦ

تِلْكَ حُدُودُ ٱللَّهِ فَلَا تَعْتَدُوهَا وَمَن يَتَعَدَّ حُدُودَ ٱللَّهِ

فَأُوْلَٰٓئِكَ هُمُ ٱلظَّٰلِمُونَ ۞ فَإِن طَلَّقَهَا فَلَا تَحِلُّ لَهُۥ مِنۢ

بَعْدُ حَتَّىٰ تَنكِحَ زَوْجًا غَيْرَهُۥ فَإِن طَلَّقَهَا فَلَا جُنَاحَ

عَلَيْهِمَآ أَن يَتَرَاجَعَآ إِن ظَنَّآ أَن يُقِيمَا حُدُودَ ٱللَّهِ

وَتِلْكَ حُدُودُ ٱللَّهِ يُبَيِّنُهَا لِقَوْمٍ يَعْلَمُونَ ۞ وَإِذَا

طَلَّقْتُمُ ٱلنِّسَآءَ فَبَلَغْنَ أَجَلَهُنَّ فَأَمْسِكُوهُنَّ بِمَعْرُوفٍ أَوْ

سَرِّحُوهُنَّ بِمَعْرُوفٍ وَلَا تُمْسِكُوهُنَّ ضِرَارًا لِّتَعْتَدُواْ وَمَن

يَفْعَلْ ذَٰلِكَ فَقَدْ ظَلَمَ نَفْسَهُۥ وَلَا تَتَّخِذُوٓاْ ءَايَٰتِ

ٱللَّهِ هُزُوًا وَٱذْكُرُواْ نِعْمَتَ ٱللَّهِ عَلَيْكُمْ وَمَآ أَنزَلَ عَلَيْكُم

مِّنَ ٱلْكِتَٰبِ وَٱلْحِكْمَةِ يَعِظُكُم بِهِۦ وَٱتَّقُواْ ٱللَّهَ وَٱعْلَمُوٓاْ

أَنَّ ٱللَّهَ بِكُلِّ شَىْءٍ عَلِيمٌ ۞ وَإِذَا طَلَّقْتُمُ ٱلنِّسَآءَ

فَبَلَغْنَ أَجَلَهُنَّ فَلَا تَعْضُلُوهُنَّ أَن يَنكِحْنَ أَزْوَٰجَهُنَّ

إِذَا تَرَٰضَوْاْ بَيْنَهُم بِٱلْمَعْرُوفِ ذَٰلِكَ يُوعَظُ بِهِۦ مَن كَانَ

"The divorce is twice, after that, either you retain her on reasonable terms or release her with kindness. And it is not lawful for you (men) to take back (from your wives) any of your *Mahr* (bridal money given by the husband to his wife at the time of marriage) which you have given them, except when both parties fear that they would be unable to keep the limits ordained by Allāh (e.g. to deal with each other on a fair basis). Then if you fear that they would not be able to keep the limits ordained by Allāh, then there is no sin on either of them if she gives back (the *Mahr* or a part of it) for her *Al-Khul'* (divorce). These are the limits ordained by Allāh, so do not transgress them. And whoever transgresses the limits ordained by Allāh, then such are the *Zâlimûn* (wrong-doers, etc.). (230) and if he has divorced her (the third time), then she is not lawful unto him after that until she has married another husband. Then, if the other husband divorces her, it is no sin on both of them that they reunite, provided they feel that they can keep the limits ordained by Allāh. These are the limits of Allāh, which He makes plain for the people who have knowledge. (231) And when you have divorced women, and they have fulfilled the term of their prescribed period, either take them back on reasonable basis or set them free on reasonable basis. But do not take them back to hurt them, and whoever does that, then he has wronged himself. And treat not the Verses (Laws) of Allāh as a jest, but remember Allāh's Favours on you (i.e. Islām), and that which He has sent down to you of the Book (i.e. the Qur'ân) and *al-Hikmah* (the Prophet's *Sunnah* - legal ways - Islāmic jurisprudence, etc.) whereby He instructs you. And fear Allāh, and know that Allāh is All-Aware of everything. (232) and when you have divorced women, and they have fulfilled the term of their prescribed period, do not prevent them from marrying their (former) husbands, if they mutually agree on reasonable basis. This (instruction) is an admonition for him among you who believes in Allāh and the Last Day. That is more virtuous and purer for you. Allāh knows, and you know not." [Sūrah al-Baqarah (2):229-232]

Second: Placing precise guidelines associated with spending on the woman in the case of her being kept in marriage or released (out of marriage) along with an encouragement to maintain kindness to her as much as possible in all situations.

Allāh (سُبْحَانَهُوَتَعَالَى) says:

لَّا جُنَاحَ عَلَيۡكُمۡ إِن طَلَّقۡتُمُ ٱلنِّسَآءَ مَا لَمۡ
تَمَسُّوهُنَّ أَوۡ تَفۡرِضُوا۟ لَهُنَّ فَرِيضَةً وَمَتِّعُوهُنَّ عَلَى

ٱلْمُوسِعِ قَدَرُهُۥ وَعَلَى ٱلْمُقْتِرِ قَدَرُهُۥ مَتَـٰعًا بِٱلْمَعْرُوفِ حَقًّا عَلَى ٱلْمُحْسِنِينَ ۞ وَإِن طَلَّقْتُمُوهُنَّ مِن قَبْلِ أَن تَمَسُّوهُنَّ وَقَدْ فَرَضْتُمْ لَهُنَّ فَرِيضَةً فَنِصْفُ مَا فَرَضْتُمْ إِلَّآ أَن يَعْفُونَ أَوْ يَعْفُوَا۟ ٱلَّذِى بِيَدِهِۦ عُقْدَةُ ٱلنِّكَاحِ وَأَن تَعْفُوٓا۟ أَقْرَبُ لِلتَّقْوَىٰ وَلَا تَنسَوُا۟ ٱلْفَضْلَ بَيْنَكُمْ إِنَّ ٱللَّهَ بِمَا تَعْمَلُونَ بَصِيرٌ ۞ ﴾

"There is no sin on you, if you divorce women while yet you have not touched (had sexual relation with) them, nor appointed unto them their *Mahr* (bridal money given by the husband to his wife at the time of marriage). But bestow on them (a suitable gift), the rich according to his means, and the poor according to his means, a gift of reasonable amount is a duty on the doers of good. And if you divorce them before you have touched (had a sexual relation with) them, and you have appointed unto them the *Mahr* (bridal money given by the husbands to his wife at the time of marriage), then pay half of that (*Mahr*), unless they (the women) agree to forego it, or he (the husband), in whose hands is the marriage tie, agrees to forego and give her full appointed *Mahr*. And to forego and give (her the full *Mahr*) is nearer to *at-Taqwa* (piety, righteousness, etc.). And do not forget liberality

**between yourselves. Truly, Allāh is All-Seer of
what you do."** [Sūrah al-Baqarah (2):236-238]

<u>Third:</u> husband is obliged to give the wife a dowry that is
agreed to by her, and if she forgoes anything from it, then it
will be permissible for him. Allāh (سُبْحَانَهُوَتَعَالَى) says:

﴿ وَءَاتُواْ ٱلنِّسَآءَ صَدُقَٰتِهِنَّ نِحْلَةً فَإِن طِبْنَ لَكُمْ عَن
شَىْءٍ مِّنْهُ نَفْسًا فَكُلُوهُ هَنِيٓـًٔا مَّرِيٓـًٔا ٤ ﴾

**"And give to the women (whom you marry) their
Mahr (obligatory bridal money given by the
husband to his wife at the time of marriage) with a
good heart, but if they, of their good pleasure, remit
any part of it to you, take it, and enjoy it without
fear of any harm (as Allāh has made it lawful)."**
[Sūrah An-Nisā' (4):4]

<u>Forth:</u> Her portion of the inheritance from that which is left
behind by her parents or other than them from her kin is
according to the type of relationship she has with that
relative and the limits that she deserves. Allāh (سُبْحَانَهُوَتَعَالَى)
says:

﴿ لِّلرِّجَالِ نَصِيبٌ مِّمَّا تَرَكَ ٱلْوَٰلِدَانِ وَٱلْأَقْرَبُونَ وَلِلنِّسَآءِ
نَصِيبٌ مِّمَّا تَرَكَ ٱلْوَٰلِدَانِ وَٱلْأَقْرَبُونَ مِمَّا قَلَّ مِنْهُ أَوْ
كَثُرَ نَصِيبًا مَّفْرُوضًا ٧ ﴾

"There is a share for men and a share for women from what is left by parents and those nearest related, whether, the property be small or large - a legal share." [Sūrah An-Nisā᾽ (4):7]

Fifth: A warning against wrongfully preventing a woman from marriage, or pressuring confining her, or returning anything of her dowry. Allāh (سُبْحَانَهُۥوَتَعَالَىٰ) says:

﴿ يَٰٓأَيُّهَا ٱلَّذِينَ ءَامَنُواْ لَا يَحِلُّ لَكُمْ أَن تَرِثُواْ ٱلنِّسَآءَ كَرْهًا ۖ وَلَا تَعْضُلُوهُنَّ لِتَذْهَبُواْ بِبَعْضِ مَآ ءَاتَيْتُمُوهُنَّ إِلَّآ أَن يَأْتِينَ بِفَٰحِشَةٍ مُّبَيِّنَةٍ ۚ وَعَاشِرُوهُنَّ بِٱلْمَعْرُوفِ ۚ فَإِن كَرِهْتُمُوهُنَّ فَعَسَىٰٓ أَن تَكْرَهُواْ شَيْئًا وَيَجْعَلَ ٱللَّهُ فِيهِ خَيْرًا كَثِيرًا ۝ وَإِنْ أَرَدتُّمُ ٱسْتِبْدَالَ زَوْجٍ مَّكَانَ زَوْجٍ وَءَاتَيْتُمْ إِحْدَىٰهُنَّ قِنطَارًا فَلَا تَأْخُذُواْ مِنْهُ شَيْئًا ۚ أَتَأْخُذُونَهُۥ بُهْتَٰنًا وَإِثْمًا مُّبِينًا ۝ وَكَيْفَ

تَأْخُذُوهُۥ وَقَدْ أَفْضَىٰ بَعْضُكُمْ إِلَىٰ بَعْضٍ وَأَخَذْنَ
مِنكُم مِّيثَٰقًا غَلِيظًا ﴿٢١﴾

"O you who believe! You are forbidden to inherit women against their will, and you should not treat them with harshness, that you may take away part of the *Mahr* you have given them, unless they commit open illegal sexual intercourse. And live with them honorably. If you dislike them, it may be that you dislike a thing, and Allāh brings through it a great deal of good. (20). But if you intend to replace a wife by another and you have given one of them a *Cantar* (of gold i.e. a great amount) as *Mahr*, take not the least bit of it back; would you take it wrongfully without a right and (with) a manifest sin? (21). And how could you take it (back) while you have gone in unto each other, and they have taken from you a firm and strong covenant?" [Sūrah An-Nisā' (4):19-21]

Sixth: Clarifying every gender's unique qualities and merits, and warning against the aspiring of one of them for what the other has been favored with. Allāh (سُبْحَانَهُ وَتَعَالَى) says:

﴿ وَلَا تَتَمَنَّوْاْ مَا فَضَّلَ ٱللَّهُ بِهِۦ بَعْضَكُمْ عَلَىٰ
بَعْضٍ لِّلرِّجَالِ نَصِيبٌ مِّمَّا ٱكْتَسَبُواْ وَلِلنِّسَآءِ نَصِيبٌ

مِّمَّا ٱكْتَسَبْنَ وَسْئَلُوا۟ ٱللَّهَ مِن فَضْلِهِ إِنَّ ٱللَّهَ كَانَ بِكُلِّ شَىْءٍ عَلِيمًا ۝

"And wish not for the things in which Allāh has made some of you to excel others. For men, there is a reward for what they have earned, (and likewise) for women there is a reward for what they have earned, and ask Allāh of His Bounty. Surely, Allāh is Ever All-Knower of everything." [Sūrah An-Nisā' (4):32]

Seventh: She has been made an associate with the man in acts of obedience and getting closer to Allāh; and has been obliged with what Allāh has commanded from the acts of worship. And on the day of Resurrection, every one of them both will have his or her reward and recompense according to their Ikhlās, seriousness and worship. Allāh (سُبْحَانَهُ وَتَعَالَى) says:

إِنَّ ٱلْمُسْلِمِينَ وَٱلْمُسْلِمَٰتِ وَٱلْمُؤْمِنِينَ وَٱلْمُؤْمِنَٰتِ وَٱلْقَٰنِتِينَ وَٱلْقَٰنِتَٰتِ وَٱلصَّٰدِقِينَ وَٱلصَّٰدِقَٰتِ وَٱلصَّٰبِرِينَ وَٱلصَّٰبِرَٰتِ وَٱلْخَٰشِعِينَ وَٱلْخَٰشِعَٰتِ وَٱلْمُتَصَدِّقِينَ وَٱلْمُتَصَدِّقَٰتِ وَٱلصَّٰٓئِمِينَ وَٱلصَّٰٓئِمَٰتِ وَٱلْحَٰفِظِينَ فُرُوجَهُمْ

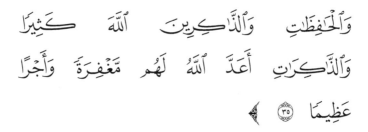

"Verily, the Muslims (those who submit to Allāh in Islām) men and women, the believers men and women (who believe in Islāmic Monotheism), the men and the women who are obedient (to Allāh), the men and women who are truthful (in their speech and deeds), the men and the women who are patient (in performing all the duties which Allāh has ordered and in abstaining from all that Allāh has forbidden), the men and the women who are humble (before their Lord Allāh), the men and the women who give *Sadaqât* (i.e. *Zakât*, and alms, etc.), the men and the women who observe *Saum* (fast) (the obligatory fasting during the month of Ramadân, and the optional *Nawâfil* fasting), the men and the women who guard their chastity (from illegal sexual acts) and the men and the women who remember Allāh much with their hearts and tongues (while sitting, standing, lying, etc. for more than 300 times extra over the remembrance of Allāh during the five compulsory congregational prayers) or praying extra additional *Nawâfil* prayers of night in the last part of night, etc.) Allāh has prepared for them forgiveness and a great reward (i.e., Paradise)." [Sūrah al-ʾAḥzāb (33) :35]

Eighth: Placing down the precise guidelines to remedy marital cruelty and desertion, or what is similar to that from discord that could possibly occur between the spouses. Allāh (سُبْحَانَهُ وَتَعَالَى) says:

﴿ وَإِنِ ٱمْرَأَةٌ خَافَتْ مِنْ بَعْلِهَا نُشُوزًا أَوْ إِعْرَاضًا فَلَا جُنَاحَ عَلَيْهِمَآ أَن يُصْلِحَا بَيْنَهُمَا صُلْحًا وَٱلصُّلْحُ خَيْرٌ وَأُحْضِرَتِ ٱلْأَنفُسُ ٱلشُّحَّ وَإِن تُحْسِنُوا۟ وَتَتَّقُوا۟ فَإِنَّ ٱللَّهَ كَانَ بِمَا تَعْمَلُونَ خَبِيرًا ۝ وَلَن تَسْتَطِيعُوٓا۟ أَن تَعْدِلُوا۟ بَيْنَ ٱلنِّسَآءِ وَلَوْ حَرَصْتُمْ فَلَا تَمِيلُوا۟ كُلَّ ٱلْمَيْلِ فَتَذَرُوهَا كَٱلْمُعَلَّقَةِ وَإِن تُصْلِحُوا۟ وَتَتَّقُوا۟ فَإِنَّ ٱللَّهَ كَانَ غَفُورًا رَّحِيمًا ۝ ﴾

"And if a woman fears cruelty or desertion on her husband's part, there is no sin on them both if they make terms of peace between themselves, and making peace is better. And human inner-selves are swayed by greed. But if you do good and keep away from evil, verily, Allāh is Ever Well-

Acquainted with what you do. You will never be able to do perfect justice between wives even if it is your ardent desire, so do not incline too much to one of them (by giving her more of your time and provision) so as to leave the other hanging (i.e. neither divorced nor married). And if you do justice and do all that is right and fear Allāh by keeping away from all that is wrong, then Allāh is Ever Oft-Forgiving, Most Merciful." [Sūrah An-Nisā' (4):128-129]

Ninth: Exposing the polytheists for their aversion to women and dispraising them to the utmost extent for that. Allāh (سُبْحَانَهُ وَتَعَالَى) says:

وَإِذَا بُشِّرَ أَحَدُهُم بِٱلْأُنثَىٰ ظَلَّ وَجْهُهُ مُسْوَدًّا وَهُوَ كَظِيمٌ ﴿٥٨﴾ يَتَوَرَىٰ مِنَ ٱلْقَوْمِ مِن سُوءِ مَا بُشِّرَ بِهِۦٓ أَيُمْسِكُهُۥ عَلَىٰ هُونٍ أَمْ يَدُسُّهُۥ فِى ٱلتُّرَابِ أَلَا سَآءَ مَا يَحْكُمُونَ ﴿٥٩﴾

"And when the news of (the birth of) a female (child) is brought to any of them, his face becomes dark, and he is filled with inward grief! He hides himself from the people because of the evil of that of what he has been informed. Shall he keep her

with dishonor or bury her in the earth? Certainly,
evil is their decision.**" [Sūrah Al-Naḥl (16):58-59]

Tenth: A warning to the utmost extent from accusing the
chaste believing women of that which they are innocent.
Allāh (سُبْحَانَهُوَتَعَالَى) says:

﴾ وَٱلَّذِينَ يَرْمُونَ ٱلْمُحْصَنَٰتِ ثُمَّ لَمْ يَأْتُواْ بِأَرْبَعَةِ
شُهَدَآءَ فَٱجْلِدُوهُمْ ثَمَٰنِينَ جَلْدَةً وَلَا تَقْبَلُواْ لَهُمْ شَهَٰدَةً
أَبَدًا وَأُوْلَٰٓئِكَ هُمُ ٱلْفَٰسِقُونَ ۝ ﴿

"**And those who accuse chaste women, and produce
not four witnesses, flog them with eighty stripes
and reject their testimony forever, they indeed are
the _Fâsiqûn_ (liars, rebellious, disobedient to
Allāh).**" [Sūrah an-Nūr (24):4]

And Allāh (سُبْحَانَهُوَتَعَالَى) says:

﴾ إِنَّ ٱلَّذِينَ يَرْمُونَ ٱلْمُحْصَنَٰتِ ٱلْغَٰفِلَٰتِ ٱلْمُؤْمِنَٰتِ
لُعِنُواْ فِى ٱلدُّنْيَا وَٱلْأَخِرَةِ وَلَهُمْ عَذَابٌ عَظِيمٌ ۝ ﴿

"**Verily, those who accuse chaste women, who
never even think of anything touching their
chastity and are good believers, are cursed in this
life and the Hereafter. And for them will be a great
torment.**" [Sūrah an-Nūr (24):23]

Eleventh: A clarification that marriage is among Allāh's great signs by which tranquility, love and mercy are established. Allāh, (سُبْحَانَهُوَتَعَالَى) says:

﴿ وَمِنْ ءَايَٰتِهِۦٓ أَنْ خَلَقَ لَكُم مِّنْ أَنفُسِكُمْ أَزْوَٰجًا لِّتَسْكُنُوٓاْ إِلَيْهَا وَجَعَلَ بَيْنَكُم مَّوَدَّةً وَرَحْمَةً إِنَّ فِى ذَٰلِكَ لَءَايَٰتٍ لِّقَوْمٍ يَتَفَكَّرُونَ ﴿٢١﴾ ﴾

"And among His Signs is this, that He created for you wives from among yourselves, that you may find repose in them, and He has put between you affection and mercy. Verily, in that are indeed signs for a people who reflect." [Sūrah Al-Rūm (30):21]

Twelfth: The placement of guidelines that are associated with divorce, the waiting period of the divorced woman, the witnesses, the spending at the time of separating, etc…Allāh (سُبْحَانَهُوَتَعَالَى) says:

﴿ يَٰٓأَيُّهَا ٱلنَّبِىُّ إِذَا طَلَّقْتُمُ ٱلنِّسَآءَ فَطَلِّقُوهُنَّ لِعِدَّتِهِنَّ وَأَحْصُواْ ٱلْعِدَّةَ وَٱتَّقُواْ ٱللَّهَ رَبَّكُمْ لَا تُخْرِجُوهُنَّ مِنۢ بُيُوتِهِنَّ وَلَا يَخْرُجْنَ إِلَّآ أَن يَأْتِينَ بِفَٰحِشَةٍ مُّبَيِّنَةٍ وَتِلْكَ حُدُودُ ٱللَّهِ وَمَن يَتَعَدَّ حُدُودَ ٱللَّهِ فَقَدْ ظَلَمَ

نَفْسَهُۥ لَا تَدْرِى لَعَلَّ ٱللَّهَ يُحْدِثُ بَعْدَ ذَٰلِكَ أَمْرًا ﴿١﴾ فَإِذَا بَلَغْنَ أَجَلَهُنَّ فَأَمْسِكُوهُنَّ بِمَعْرُوفٍ أَوْ فَارِقُوهُنَّ بِمَعْرُوفٍ وَأَشْهِدُواْ ذَوَىْ عَدْلٍ مِّنكُمْ وَأَقِيمُواْ ٱلشَّهَٰدَةَ لِلَّهِ ذَٰلِكُمْ يُوعَظُ بِهِۦ مَن كَانَ يُؤْمِنُ بِٱللَّهِ وَٱلْيَوْمِ ٱلْءَاخِرِ وَمَن يَتَّقِ ٱللَّهَ يَجْعَل لَّهُۥ مَخْرَجًا ﴿٢﴾

"O Prophet! When you divorce women, divorce them at their 'Iddah (prescribed periods) and count (accurately) their 'Iddah (periods). And fear Allāh your Lord (O Muslims), and turn them not out of their (husband's) homes, nor shall they (themselves) leave, except in case they are guilty of some open illegal sexual intercourse. And those are the set limits of Allāh. And whosoever transgresses the set limits of Allāh, then indeed he has wronged himself. You (the one who divorces his wife) know not, it may be that Allāh will afterward bring some new thing to pass (i.e. to return her back to you if that was the first or second divorce). Then when they are about to fulfill their term appointed, either take them back in a good manner or part with them in a proper way. And take for witness two just persons from among you (Muslims). And establish the witness for Allāh. That will be an admonition

given to him who believes in Allāh and the Last
Day. And whosoever fears Allāh and keeps his duty
to Him, He will make a way for him to get out (from
every difficulty)." [Sūrah at-Talāq (65):1-2]

And He (سُبْحَانَهُوَتَعَالَى) says:

﴿ أَسْكِنُوهُنَّ مِنْ حَيْثُ سَكَنتُم مِّن وُجْدِكُمْ وَلَا تُضَآرُّوهُنَّ
لِتُضَيِّقُواْ عَلَيْهِنَّ وَإِن كُنَّ أُوْلَٰتِ حَمْلٍ فَأَنفِقُواْ عَلَيْهِنَّ حَتَّىٰ
يَضَعْنَ حَمْلَهُنَّ فَإِنْ أَرْضَعْنَ لَكُمْ فَـَٔاتُوهُنَّ أُجُورَهُنَّ وَأْتَمِرُواْ
بَيْنَكُم بِمَعْرُوفٍ وَإِن تَعَاسَرْتُمْ فَسَتُرْضِعُ لَهُۥ أُخْرَىٰ ٦ ﴾

"Lodge them (the divorced women) where you
dwell, according to your means, and do not treat
them in such a harmful way that they are obliged
to leave. And if they are pregnant, then spend on
them till they deliver. Then if they give suck to the
children for you, give them their due payment, and
let each of you accept the advice of the other in a
just way. But if you make difficulties for one
another, then some other woman may give suck for
him (the father of the child)." [Soorah at-Talaaq
65:6]

Thirteenth: Polygyny has been limited to a number of four wives for those who desire it with the stipulation to be just. Allāh (سُبْحَانَهُ وَتَعَالَى) says:

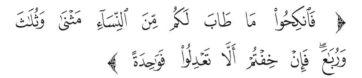

"Then marry (other) women of your choice, two or three, or four but if you fear that you shall not be able to deal justly (with them), then only one."
[Sūrah An-Nisā' (4):3]

These are some examples of the Noble Qur'ān's guidance regarding the woman and kindness to her; and also regarding the guidelines that one must abide by when dealing with her. These are wise guidelines and straight directives that if not abided by and strictly adhered to, the peoples' conditions would be unmanaged and their affairs unstraitened; for they are a revelation from the Lord of all that exists, the All-Knowing of His creation and All-Wise of His Legislation.

THE RECEPTION FOR THE WOMAN UNDER THE SHADE OF ISLĀM

Surely, the Muslim woman under the shade of Islām's upright teachings and wise directives lives an honored life filled with salutations and respect from the first day she is brought into this life: she passes through all the circumstances in her life as either a daughter, mother, wife, sister, paternal aunt, or a maternal aunt; and in every one of these situations, she has exclusive rights and a portion of hospitality and honor that is due to her.

In her role as a daughter: Indeed, the religion of Islām calls to beneficence towards her, great consideration for her upbringing and care, and excellent cultivation of her etiquettes so that she is brought up as a righteous, guarded, chaste woman. Islām condemns the people of the pre-Islāmic era for their burying their daughters and disliking her birth. Allāh (سُبْحَانَهُوَتَعَالَى) says:

﴿ وَإِذَا بُشِّرَ أَحَدُهُم بِٱلْأُنثَىٰ ظَلَّ وَجْهُهُۥ مُسْوَدًّا وَهُوَ كَظِيمٌ ۝ يَتَوَرَىٰ مِنَ ٱلْقَوْمِ مِن سُوٓءِ مَا بُشِّرَ بِهِۦٓ أَيُمْسِكُهُۥ عَلَىٰ هُونٍ أَمْ يَدُسُّهُۥ فِى ٱلتُّرَابِ أَلَا سَآءَ مَا يَحْكُمُونَ ۝ ﴾

"And when the news of (the birth of) a female (child) is brought to any of them, his face becomes dark, and he is filled with inward grief! He hides himself from the people because of the evil of that of what he has been informed. Shall he keep her with dishonor or bury her in the earth? Certainly, evil is their decision." [Sūrah Al-Naḥl (16):58-59]

It is mentioned in the *Ṣaḥīḥ* of al-Bukhārī and Muslim on the authority of al-Mughayrah ibn Shu'bah (رَضِيَٱللَّهُعَنْه) that the Prophet (صَلَّىٱللَّهُعَلَيْهِوَسَلَّم) said:

$$ إِنَّ اللهَ حَرَّمَ عَلَيْكُمْ عُقُوقَ الْأُمَّهَاتِ ، وَ مَنْعـاً $$

$$ وهات ، وَ وَأْدَ الْـبَـنَـاتِ .... $$

"Allāh has forbidden for you to be disobedient to your mother, to withhold (what you should give), or demand (what you do not deserve), and to bury your daughters alive.." [15]

al-Hafidh ibn Hajar (رَحِمَهُٱللَّه) mentioned that the people of *Jaahiliyyah* (i.e., Pre-Islāmic era of ignorance) would bury their daughters in one of two ways:

---

[15] al-Bukhārī reported it (5975); and Muslim reported it (593).

First way: The husband would order his wife when she was nearing delivery to give birth next to a ditch. If she gave birth to a boy, she would keep it; and if she gave birth to a girl, she would toss her in the ditch.

Second way Some of the men, when their daughter became six years old, would say to her mother, "Perfume her and beautify her as I am going to take her to visit our kin." He would then take her out to the desert until he arrives at a well, and say to her, "Look at the well," after which he would push her into it from behind and cover the well. [16]

The religion of Islām has deemed the woman a tremendous blessing and a noble gift from Allāh (جَلَّوَعَلَا),

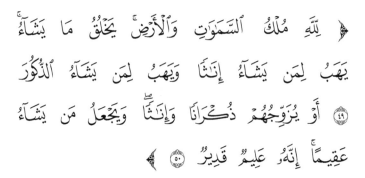

"To Allāh belongs the kingdom of the heavens and the earth. He creates what He wills. He bestows

---

[16] Refer to the book, *"Fath-ul-Baari"* (10/421).

female (offspring) upon whom He wills and bestows male (offspring) upon whom He wills. Or He bestows both males and females, and He renders barren whom He wills. Verily, He is the All-Knower and can do all things." [Sūrah ash-Shurā' (42):49-50]

Allāh urges us to be concerned with her etiquettes, nurturing, and education. In the *Musnad* of al-Imām Ahmad, the Prophet (ﷺ) said,

مَنْ كَانَتْ لَهُ أُنثى فَلَمْ يَئِدْهَا، وَ لَمْ يُهِنْهَا، وَ لَمْ يؤْثِرْ وَلَدَهُ عَلَيْهَا أَدْخَلَهُ اللهُ تَعَالَى الْجَنَّةَ.

"If anyone has a female child, and does not bury her alive, or insults her, or prefer his children (i.e., the male ones) to her, Allāh will enter him into Paradise." [17]

Ibn Mājah reported on the authority of 'Aqbah Ibn 'Aamir (ﺭﺿﻲ ﺍﻟﻠﻪ ﻋﻨﻪ) that he said, "I heard the Messenger of Allāh (ﷺ) say,

---

[17] *Musnad Ahmad* (1/223).

مَنْ كَانَ لَهُ ثَلَاثُ بَنَاتٍ وَ صَبَرَ عَلَيْهِنَّ ، وَ
كَسَاهُنَّ مِنْ جِدَتِهِ ، كُنَّ لَهُ حِجَاباً مِنَ النَّارِ

"If someone has three daughters and is patient with them and clothes them from his wealth, they will be a shield against the Fire for him." [18]

Imam Muslim reported in his Ṣaḥīḥ that the Prophet (ﷺ) said:

مَنْ عَالَ جَارِيَتَيْنِ حَتَّى تَبْلُغَا، جَاءَ يَوْمَ
الْقِيَامَةِ أَنَا وَ هُوَ كَهَاتَيْنِ . وَ ضَمَّ أَصَابِعَهُ .

"Whoever raises two or three daughters until they are grown; Him and I will be like this" and He placed his fingers together. [19]

Al-Imām Ahmad reported the Prophet (ﷺ) said:

---

[18] *Sunan Ibn Majah* (#3669).

[19] *Ṣaḥīḥ Muslim* (2631).

مَنْ عَالَ ابْنَتَيْنِ أَوْ ثَلَاثَ بَنَاتٍ ، أَوْ أُخْتَيْنِ ، أَوْ

ثَلَاثَ أَخَوَاتٍ ، حَتَّى يَبْلُغْنَ ، أَوْ يَمُوتَ عَنْهُنَّ ،

أَنَا وَ هُوَ كَهَاتَيْنِ . وَ أَشَارَ بِإِصْبَعِهِ السَّبَّابَةِ .

"Whoever raises two or three daughters, or two or three sisters until they are grown, or he dies; Him and I will be like this" and He pointed with his index finger. [20]

al-Bukhārī reported in his book, *al-Adab Mufrad*, on the authority of Jaabir Ibn ''Abdullah that he said, "The Messenger (ﷺ) said:

مَنْ كَانَ لَهُ ثَلَاثُ بَنَاتٍ يُؤْوِيهِنَّ وَ يكفِيهِنَّ

وَ يَرْحَمُهُنَّ ، فَقَدْ وَجَبَتْ لَهُ الْجَنَّةُ الْبَتَّةَ .

فَقَالَ رَجُلٌ مِنْ بَعْضِ الْقَوْمِ : وَ ثِنْتَيْنِ يَا

رَسُولَ اللهِ؟ قَالَ : وَ ثِنْتَيْنِ

"'Anyone who has three daughters and provides for them, clothes them and shows mercy to them will undoubtedly enter the Garden.' A man from

---

[20] *Musnad Ahmad* (3/148)

the people said, 'and two daughters, O Messenger
of Allāh?' He said, 'and two.'" [21]

In Ṣaḥīḥ al-Bukhārī and Muslim is the Ḥadīth on the
authority of ʿĀʾishah (رَضِيَاللَّهُعَنْهَا) who said:

جَاءَ أَعْرَابِيٌّ إِلَى النَّبِيِّ صَلَّى اللهُ عَلَيْهِ وَ

سَلَّمَ فَقَالَ : أَ تُقَبِّلُونَ صِبْيَانَكُمْ ؟ فَمَا

نُقَبِّلُهُمْ ، فَقَالَ النَّبِيُّ صَلَّى اللهُ عَلَيْهِ وَ

سَلَّمَ : ((أَوْ أَمْلِكُ لَكَ أَنْ نَزَعَ اللهُ مِنْ قَلْبِكَ

الرَّحْمَةَ)) .

"a bedouin came to the Prophet (صَلَّىاللَّهُعَلَيْهِوَسَلَّمَ) and
asked, 'Do you kiss your children? We do not kiss
them.' After that the Prophet (صَلَّىاللَّهُعَلَيْهِوَسَلَّمَ) said:
'Then what can I do if Allāh has deprived you of
mercy?'" [22]

In her role as a mother: Islām calls for honoring the woman
with a special and tremendous honor in her role as a mother
through goodness and kindness to her, taking steps towards

---

[21] *Al-Adaab al-Mufrad* (178).

[22] *Ṣaḥīḥ al-Bukhārī* (5998); and *Ṣaḥīḥ Muslim* (2317).

being at her service, supplicating for her, not exposing her to any type of harm, and treating her as the most excellent and virtuous companion. Allāh (سُبْحَانَهُۥوَتَعَالَىٰ) says:

﴿ وَوَصَّيْنَا ٱلْإِنسَٰنَ بِوَٰلِدَيْهِ إِحْسَٰنًا حَمَلَتْهُ أُمُّهُۥ كُرْهًا وَوَضَعَتْهُ كُرْهًا وَحَمْلُهُۥ وَفِصَٰلُهُۥ ثَلَٰثُونَ شَهْرًا حَتَّىٰ إِذَا بَلَغَ أَشُدَّهُۥ وَبَلَغَ أَرْبَعِينَ سَنَةً قَالَ رَبِّ أَوْزِعْنِىٓ أَنْ أَشْكُرَ نِعْمَتَكَ ٱلَّتِىٓ أَنْعَمْتَ عَلَىَّ وَعَلَىٰ وَٰلِدَىَّ وَأَنْ أَعْمَلَ صَٰلِحًا تَرْضَىٰهُ وَأَصْلِحْ لِى فِى ذُرِّيَّتِىٓ إِنِّى تُبْتُ إِلَيْكَ وَإِنِّى مِنَ ٱلْمُسْلِمِينَ ۝ ﴾

"And We have enjoined man to be dutiful and kind to his parents. His mother bears him with hardship, and she brings him forth with hardship, and the bearing of him and the weaning of him is thirty (30) months, till when he attains full strength and reaches forty years, he says: "My Lord! Grant me the power and ability that I may be grateful for Your Favour that You have bestowed upon me and my parents, and that I may do righteous good deeds, such as please You, and make my off-spring good. Indeed, I have turned to You in repentance, and truly, I am one of the Muslims (submitting to Your Will)." [Sūrah al-Aḥqāf (46):15]

And Allāh (سُبْحَانَهُوَتَعَالَىٰ) says:

وَقَضَىٰ رَبُّكَ أَلَّا تَعْبُدُوٓاْ إِلَّآ إِيَّاهُ وَبِٱلْوَٰلِدَيْنِ إِحْسَٰنًا إِمَّا يَبْلُغَنَّ عِندَكَ ٱلْكِبَرَ أَحَدُهُمَآ أَوْ كِلَاهُمَا فَلَا تَقُل لَّهُمَآ أُفٍّ وَلَا تَنْهَرْهُمَا وَقُل لَّهُمَا قَوْلًا كَرِيمًا ۝ وَٱخْفِضْ لَهُمَا جَنَاحَ ٱلذُّلِّ مِنَ ٱلرَّحْمَةِ وَقُل رَّبِّ ٱرْحَمْهُمَا كَمَا رَبَّيَانِي صَغِيرًا

"And your Lord has decreed that you worship none
but Him. And that you be dutiful to your parents.
If one of them or both of them attain old age in your
life, say not to them a word of disrespect, nor shout
at them but address them in terms of honor. And
lower unto them the wing of submission and
humility through mercy, and say: 'My Lord!
Bestow on them Your Mercy as they did bring me
up when I was small.'" [Sūrah Al-ʾIsrāʾ (17):23-24]

In *Ṣaḥīḥ al-Bukhārī* and *Muslim* on the authority of Abū
Hurairah (رَضِيَٱللَّهُعَنْهُ) who said, "The Messenger was asked:

يَا رَسُولَ اللهِ مَنْ أَبَرُّ؟ قَالَ : أُمَّكَ ، قَالَ : ثُمَّ مَنْ

؟ قَالَ : أُمَّكَ ، قَالَ : ثُمَّ مَنْ ؟ قَالَ : أَبَاكَ .

'O Messenger of Allāh, to whom should I be more dutiful? He said, 'your mother.' Then he asked, Then who?' The Messenger of Allāh said, 'your mother.' Then he asked again, 'then who?' the Messenger of Allāh said, 'your father.'" 23

Abū Daawood and Ibn Majah reported on the authority of ʿAbdullāh Ibn ʿUmar (رَضِيَاللهُعَنْهُ) that he said:

جَاءَ رَجُلٌ إِلَى النَّبِيِّ صَلَّى اللهُ عَلَيْهِ وَسَلَّمَ

يُبَايِعُهُ عَلَى الْهِجْرَةِ، وَتَرَكَ أَبَوَيْهِ يَبْكِيَانِ

، فَقَالَ : ((ارْجَعْ إِلَيْهِمَا وَ أَضْحِكْهُمَا كَمَا

أَبْكَيْتَهُمَا)) .

"A man came to the Prophet (صَلَّىاللهُعَلَيْهِوَسَلَّمَ) to make a pledge to him to migrate, and he left his parents crying. The Prophet said (to him), 'Return back to

---

23 *Ṣaḥīḥ al-Bukhārī* (5971); and *Muslim* (2548).

them and make them laugh as you made them cry.'" [24]

In *Ṣaḥīḥ al-Bukhārī* and *Muslim* on the authority of 'Abdullāh Ibn Mas'ūd (رَضِيَاللهُعَنْهُ) that he said:

$$سَـأَلْـتُ الـنَّـبِيَّ صَـلَّى اللهُ عَـلَـيْهِ وَ سَـلَّـمَ أَيُّ الْـعَـمَـلِ أَحَـبُّ إِلَى اللهِ عَـزَّ وَ جَلَّ ؟ قَـالَ : ((الـصَّـلَاةُ عَـلَى وَقْـتِـهَا، قُـلْـتُ : ثُـمَّ أَيّ ؟ قَـالَ : بِـرُّ الْـوَالِـدَيْـنِ، قُـلْـتُ : ثُـمَّ أَيّ ؟ قَـالَ : الْـجِهَـادُ فِي سَـبِيلِ اللهِ)).$$

"I asked the Prophet (ﷺ), 'Which deed is most beloved to Allāh?' He answered, 'The prayer performed in its fixed time.' Then I asked, 'Then which deed after that?' He answered, 'Righteousness to the parents.' Then I asked, "Then which?' He answered, 'Jihaad in the path of Allāh.'" [25]

The religion of Islām warns against harming the parents or causing them any type of injury: Doing so is deemed to be an act of disobedience that the person will be held

---

[24] *Abū Dawood* (2528) and *Ibn Maajah* (2782).

[25] *Ṣaḥīḥ al-Bukhārī* (5970) and *Muslim* (85).

accountable for on the day of Resurrection—it is an act among the major sins.

In *Ṣaḥīḥ al-Bukhārī* and *Muslim* on the authority Abū Bakrah (رَضِيَاللَّهُعَنْهُ) who said:

أَ لَا أُنَبِّئُكُمْ بِأَكْبَرِ الْكَبَائِرِ؟ ثَلَاثاً . قَالُوا : بَلَى يَا رَسُولَ اللهِ ، قَالَ : ((الْإِشْرَاكُ بِاللهِ ، وَ عُقُوقُ الْوَالِدَيْنِ ، وَ جَلَسَ وَ كَانَ مُتَّكِئاً فَقَالَ: أَلَا وَ قَوْلُ الزُّورِ)) مَا زَالَ يُكَرِّرُهَا حَتَّى قُلْنَا: لَيْتَهُ سَكَتَ .

"The Messenger of Allāh (صَلَّىاللَّهُعَلَيْهِوَسَلَّمَ) said thrice, 'Should I not inform you of the greatest of sins?' they said, 'Indeed, O Messenger of Allāh.' He said, 'Associating partners with Allāh and disobedience to the parents.' He was reclining, then he sat up and said, 'Bearing false witness;' and he continued repeating it until we wished he should become silent." [26]

---

[26] *Ṣaḥīḥ al-Bukhārī* (5976) and *Muslim* (87).

Muslim reported in his *Ṣaḥīḥ* on the authority of 'Ali
(رَضِيَاللَّهُعَنْهُ) who said:

**"The Messenger of Allāh (صَلَّىاللَّهُعَلَيْهِوَسَلَّمَ) said, 'May
Allāh curse the one who curses his parents.'"** 27

In her role as a wife: The religion of Islām encourages
honoring the woman in her role as a wife. It has given her
tremendous rights which her husband must fulfill; and he
similarly has enormous rights upon her. Among the wife's
rights in Islām are the following: to live with her in a good
fasion, kindness to her by providing her with food, drink, and
clothing, being gentle, hospitable and patient towards her, as
well as treating her honorably. In the religion of Islām, the
most excellent among the people are those who are best to
their family. Also from her rights is that he (the spouse) teach
her the religion, have jealousy for her, protect her dignity and
live with her in a most-excellent manner.

Among the verses that summarize the rights of the wife is
Allāh's statement:

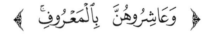

---

27 *Ṣaḥīḥ Muslim* (1978).

"And live with them honorably." [Sūrah An-Nisā᾽ (4):19]

Numerous narrations are mentioned in the Sunnah emphasizing deference to the rights of the wife and care for her. Among these is what is affirmed in the Ṣaḥīḥ of al-Bukhārī and Muslim on the authority of Abū Hurairah (رَضِيَاللَّهُعَنْهُ) who said:

اسْـتَـوْصُـوا بِـالـنِّـسَـاءِ خَـيْـراً ، فَـإِنَّ الْـمَـرْأَةَ خُـلِـقَـتْ

مِـنْ ضِـلْـعٍ أَعْـوَجَ ، وَ إِنَّ أَعْـوَجَ شَـيْءٍ فِـي الـضِّـلْـعِ

أَعْـلَاهُ ، فَـإِنْ ذَهَـبْـتَ تُـقِـيـمُـهُ كَـسَـرْتَـهُ ، وَ إِنْ

تَـرَكْتَـهُ لَـمْ يَـزلْ أَعْـوَجَ ، فَـاسْـتَـوْصُـوا بِـالـنِّـسَـاءِ .

"The Messenger of Allāh (صَلَّىاللَّهُعَلَيْهِوَسَلَّمَ) said, 'Act kindly towards women; for verily, the woman is created from a rib, and the most crooked part of the rib is its top. If you attempt to straighten it, you will break it. And if you leave it, its crookedness will remain there. So act kindly towards women.'"[28]

an-Nawawi (رَحِمَهُاللَّهُ) said about the Ḥadīth:

---

[28] Ṣaḥīḥ al-Bukhārī (3331) and Muslim (1468).

"Within this Ḥadīth is subtleness to women, beneficence to them, patience upon the crookedness of their character, forbearance towards the weakness of their intellect, dislike of divorcing them without any reason, and that he does not aspire to straighten her. Allāh knows best." [29]

Al-Imām Ahmad, Abū Dāwūd, and at-Tirmidhī reported from the Ḥadīth of Abū Hurairah (رَضِيَٱللَّهُعَنْهُ) that he said:

أَكْمَلُ الْمُؤْمِنِينَ إِيمَاناً أَحْسَنُهُمْ خُلُقاً ،
وَ خِيَارُكُمْ خِيَارُكُمْ لِنِسَائِهِمْ .

"The Messenger of Allāh (صَلَّىٱللَّهُعَلَيْهِوَسَلَّمَ) said, 'A perfect believer in faith is the one who is most excellent in character, and the best among you are the ones who are best to their wives." [30]

Imām Muslim reported in his *Ṣaḥīḥ* on the authority of Jābir Ibn 'Abdullāh (رَضِيَٱللَّهُعَنْهُ) that the Messenger of Allāh (صَلَّىٱللَّهُعَلَيْهِوَسَلَّمَ) said during his farewell sermon:

---

[29] Explanation of *Ṣaḥīḥ Muslim* (10/57).

[30] Imam Ahmad (2/250,472); Abū Dawud (4682); and at-Tirmidhī (1162).

فَاتَّقُوا اللهَ فِي النِّسَاءِ ، فَإِنَّكُمْ أَخَذْتُمُوهُنَّ
بِأَمَانَةِ اللهِ ، وَاسْتَحْلَلْتُمْ فُرُوجَهُنَّ بِكَلِمَةِ
اللهِ ، وَ لَكُمْ عَلَيْهِنَّ أَنْ لَا يُوطِئن فرشكُمْ
أَحَداً تَكْرَهُونَهُ فَإِنْ فَعَلْنَ ذَلِكَ فَاضْرِبُوهُنَّ
ضَرْباً غَيْرَ مُبَرِّحٍ ، وَ لَهُنَّ رِزْقُهُنَّ وَ
كِسْوَتُهُنَّ بِالْمَعْرُوفِ .

"Fear Allāh with regard to women, for you have taken them as a trust from Allāh; and intimacy with them has become permissible to you through Allāh's Word. Your rights over them are that they should not allow anyone whom you dislike sitting on your bedding. If they do that, then hit them, but in a manner that does not cause injury or leave a mark. Their rights over you are that you should provide for them and clothe them in a reasonable manner." [31]

What is intended by the statement, **"they should not allow anyone whom you dislike sitting on your bedding,"** is to not let anyone whom you dislike to enter and sit in your home whether it is a man or a woman.

---

[31] *Ṣaḥīḥ Muslim* (1218).

Muslim also reported in his *Ṣaḥīḥ* from the Ḥadīth of Abū Hurairah (رَضِيَاللَّهُعَنْهُ) that the Messenger of Allāh (صَلَّىاللَّهُعَلَيْهِوَسَلَّمَ) said:

$$\text{لَا يَفْرُكُ مُؤْمِنٌ مُؤْمِنَةً ، إِنْ كَرِهَ مِنْهَا خُلُقاً}$$

$$\text{رَضِيَ مِنْهَا آخَرَ.}$$

"A believing man should not hate a believing woman; if he dislikes one of her characteristics, he will be pleased with another." [32]

The meaning of the statement, **"should not hate,"** is that one should not loathe. So if one finds with his wife a character which he does not like and is not pleased with, then [he should remember that] within her are noble characteristics and honorable conducts more abundant.

Imam Ahmad, Abū Daawood, and at-Tirmidhi reported on the authority of ʿĀʾishah (رَضِيَاللَّهُعَنْهَا) that the Messenger of Allāh (صَلَّىاللَّهُعَلَيْهِوَسَلَّمَ) said:

$$\text{إِنَّمَا النِّسَاءُ شَقَائِقُ الرِّجَالِ.}$$

---

[32] *Ṣaḥīḥ Muslim* (1469).

"Women are the counterpart of men." [33]

Ibn al-Atheer said in his book, *an-Nihaayah,*

> **"They, men and women, are equal and the same in relation to morals and disposition; it is as though women split from men because Hawaa was created from Aadam** (عَلَيْهِٱلسَّلَامْ). **And the full brother of a man has the same father and mother as him."** [34]

Within this Ḥadīth is a call to goodness in social intercourse, wholesome interactions, subtleness, and excellence that is quite-apparent.

In her role as a sister, paternal and maternal aunt: The religion of Islām enjoins that the woman be taken care of whether she is a sister, paternal or maternal aunt; and orders to keep ties with her, to treat her with excellence, and be aware cognizant of her rights—resulting in the earning of a tremendous recompense and an abundant reward.

al-Bukhārī reported in the book, *al-Adab al-Mufrad,* as well as Ibn Maajah on the authority of al-Miqdam Ibn Ma'di Karb that he heard the Messenger of Allāh (صَلَّىٱللَّهُعَلَيْهِوَسَلَّمَ) say:

---

[33] Imām Ahmad (6/256,277); Abū Dawud (236); and at-Tirmidhi (113).

[34] *an-Nihaayah* by ibn al-Atheer (2/492).

إِنَّ اللهَ يُوصِيكُمْ بِأُمَّهَاتِكُمْ ، ثُمَّ يُوصِيكُمْ بِأُمَّهَاتِكُمْ ، ثُمَّ يُوصِيكُمْ بِآبَائِكُمْ ، ثُمَّ يُوصِيكُمْ بِالْأَقْرَبِ فَالْأَقْرَبِ .

"Allāh enjoins you to be dutiful to your mothers. Then He enjoins you to be dutiful to your mothers. Then He enjoins you to be dutiful to your fathers. Then He enjoins you to be dutiful to your next closest relative and then the next." [35]

at-Tirmidhī and Abū Dāwūd reported on the authority of Abū Saʿīd al-Khudrī that the Messenger of Allāh (صَلَّىٰاللَّهُعَلَيْهِوَسَلَّمَ) said:

لَا يَكُونُ لِأَحَدٍ ثَلَاثُ بَنَاتٍ أَوْ ثَلَاثُ أَخَوَاتٍ فَيُحْسِنُ إِلَيْهِنَّ إِلَّا دَخَلَ الْجَنَّةَ .

---

[35] al-Bukhārī reported it in his book *al-Adaab al-Mufrad* (60) and Ibn Mājah (3661).

"No one has three daughters or three sisters and is good to them except that he will enter the Garden." 36

In Ṣaḥīḥ al-Bukhārī and Muslim on the authority of ʿĀ'ishah (رَضِيَٱللَّهُعَنْهَا) that the Prophet (صَلَّىٱللَّهُعَلَيْهِوَسَلَّمَ) said:

الـرَّحِـمُ شَـجَنَـةٌ مِـنَ اللهِ ، مَـنْ وَصَـلَـهَا وَصَـلَـهُ اللهُ ، وَ مَـنْ قَـطَـعَـهَا قَـطَـعَـهُ اللهُ .

"The womb is named after ar-Rahman, so whoever keeps ties with it, Allāh will keep ties with him, and whoever severs ties with it, Allāh will sever ties with him." 37

Additionally, in Ṣaḥīḥ al-Bukhārī *and* Muslim on the authority of Anas Ibn Mālik (رَضِيَٱللَّهُعَنْهُ) that the Messenger of Allāh (صَلَّىٱللَّهُعَلَيْهِوَسَلَّمَ) said:

مَـنْ أَحَـبَّ أَنْ يُبْـسَـطَ لَـهُ فِي رِزْقِـهِ، وَ أَنْ يُـنْـسَـأَ لَـهُ فِـي أَثَرِهِ، فَـلْـيَـصِـلْ رَحِـمَهُ .

---

36 at-Tirmidhi (1912) and Abū Dawud (5147).

37 Ṣaḥīḥ al-Bukhārī (5989) and Muslim (2555).

"He who desires ample provisions and his life be prolonged, should maintain good ties with his blood relations." [38]

Her role as a foreigner to the man: If the woman is a foreigner to the man (i.e., she is not his relative) and is in need of assistance and support, then the religion of Islām encourages deference and kindness to her, as well as support that result in high rewards.

In *Ṣaḥīḥ al-Bukhārī* and *Muslim*, the Prophet (ﷺ) said:

السَّاعِي عَلَى الْأَرْمِلَةِ وَ الْمِسْكِينِ
كَالْمُجَاهِدِ فِي سَبِيلِ اللهِ أَوْ كَالْقَائِمِ الَّذِي
لَا يَفْتُرُ، أَوْ كَالصَّائِمِ الَّذِي لَا يُفْطِرُ.

"One who strives to help the widows and the poor is like the one who fights in the way of Allāh, or as the one who stands up (for prayer) without rest and as the one who observes fasts continuously." [39]

---

[38] *Ṣaḥīḥ al-Bukhārī* (5986) and *Muslim* (2557).

[39] *Ṣaḥīḥ al-Bukhārī* (6007) and *Muslim* (2982).

These are a few salutations and honors that the woman acquires under the shade of Islām's teachings. And it is absolutely out of the question that the woman can find the likes of this great concern, splendid honor, and profound beneficence given to her—or anything close to it—outside of this great religion of Allāh that He is pleased with for His servants.

JEALOUSY FOR THE MUSLIM WOMAN [40]

Surely, from the splendid forms of Islām's tribute to the Muslim woman—which is implanted in the souls of the Muslims—is having jealosy for one's *Mahaarim*[41] This is a tremendous characteristic and a noble attribute that is established within the heart of the Muslim man compelling him to care for his close relatives, to safeguard them and preserve their dignity and honor; also, it causes him to prevent them from improperly dressing, unveiling their faces and intermingling with the opposite sex.

The religion of Islām deems defending the good reputation of and having jealsoy for one's female close-relative as a form of Jihād for which he will his blood and sacrifice himself in its path; and the performer of thus is awarded the rank of a martyr in Paradise. On the authority of Sa'eed Ibn Zayd (رَضِيَاللهُعَنهُ) that he said,

---

[40] Taken from the book, *The Return of the Hijaab,* by Shaykh Muhammad bin Ahmad Isma'eel al-Muqaddim [3rd section] (pages 114-122).

[41] **TN:** close female relatives, i.e., their wives.

سَمِعْتُ رَسُولَ اللهِ صَلَّى اللهُ عَلَيْهِ وَ سَلَّمَ
يَقُولُ: مَنْ قُتِلَ دُونَ مَالِهِ فَهُوَ شَهِيدٌ، وَ مَنْ
قُتِلَ دُونَ دَمِهِ فَهُوَ شَهِيدٌ، وَ مَنْ قُتِلَ دُونَ
دِينِهِ فَهُوَ شَهِيدٌ، وَ مَنْ قُتِلَ دُونَ أَهْلِهِ فَهُوَ
شَهِيدٌ. وَ فِي لَفْظٍ: مَنْ مَاتَ دُونَ عِرضِهِ فَهُوَ
شَهِيدٌ.

"I heard the Messenger of Allāh (ﷺ) say, 'He who is killed while protecting his property is a martyr, and he who is killed while defending his blood is a martyr, and he who is killed while defending his religion is a martyr, and he who is killed while defending his family is a martyr.'" And in another wording is, "Whoever dies while defending his honor is a martyr." [42]

Rather, the religion of Islām actually deems such a jealousy to be from the core characteristics of true 'Īmān. On the authority of al-Mugheerah Ibn Shu'bah (رضي الله عنه) who said:

---

[42] Abū Daawood reported it (4772) and at-Tirmidhee (1420).

قَالَ سَعْدُ بْنُ عُبَادَةَ : لَوْ رَأَيْتُ رَجُلاً مَعَ
امْرَأَتِي لَضَرَبْتُهُ بِالسَّيْفِ غَيْرَ مصفح .
فَبَلَغَ ذَلِكَ رَسُولَ اللهِ صَلَّى اللهُ عَلَيْهِ وَ سَلَّمَ
فَقَالَ : ((تَعْجَبُونَ مِنْ غَيْرَةِ سَعْدٍ؟ لَأَنَا
أَغْيَرُ مِنْهُ ، وَاللهُ أَغْيَرُ مِنِّي ، وَ مِنْ أَجَلِ
غَيْرَةِ اللهِ حَرَّمَ الْفَوَاحِشَ مَا ظَهَرَ مِنْهَا وَ مَا
بَطَنَ .

"Sa'ad Ibn 'Ibaadah said, 'If I see a man with my wife, I will struck him with the sword, and not with the flat part (side) of it. When Allāh's Messenger (ﷺ) heard of that, he said: Are you surprised at Sa'ad's jealousy [for his woman]? By Allāh, I am more jealous than him although Allāh is more jealous than I. Because of His jealousy, Allāh has prohibited what is apparent and hidden from wickedness." [43]

On the authority of Abū Hurairah (ﺭﺿﻲ ﺍﻟﻠﻪ ﻋﻨﻪ) that the Messenger of Allāh (ﷺ) said:

---

[43] *Ṣaḥīḥ al-Bukhārī* (6846) and *Muslim* (1499).

إِنَّ اللهَ يَـغَـارُ ، وَ إِنَّ الْـمُـؤْمِـنَ يَـغَـارُ ، وَ إِنَّ مِـنْ
غَـيْـرَةِ اللهِ أَنْ يَـأْتِـيَ الْـمُـؤْمِنُ مَا حَرَّمَ اللهُ عَلَـيْـهِ

"Verily, Allāh can be jelous, and a believer can also be jelous; and from what incur's Allāh jealousy is that a believer does what Allāh has forbidden him to do." [44]

The opposite of a *"ĝhayūr"* (the very jealous) is a *"dayyūth"* (a cuckold), a person that approves wickedness for his wife and thus has no jealousy for them; and such a person has been threatened severly in the texts of the Qur'ān and Sunnah. On the authority of 'Abdullāh Ibn 'Umar (رَضِيَاللّٰهُعَنْهُمَا) who said that, "The Messenger of Allāh (صَلَّىاللّٰهُعَلَيْهِوَسَلَّمَ) said:

ثَـلَاثَـةٌ لَا يَـنْـظُـرُ اللهُ عَـزَّ وَ جَـلَّ إِلَـيْـهِمْ يَـوْمَ
الْـقِـيَـامَـةِ : الْـعَـاقُ لِـوَالِـدَيْـهِ ، وَ الْـمَـرْأَةُ
الْـمُـتَـرَجِّـلَـةُ ، وَالـدَّيُّـوثُ .

'There are three at whom Allāh (عَزَّوَجَلَّ) will not look at on the Day of Resurrection: The one who

---

[44] *Ṣaḥīḥ al-Bukhārī* (5223) and *Muslim* (2761).

disobeys his parents, the woman who imitates men in her outward appearance, and the cuckold.'"[45]

Among the incredible occurrences regarding this matter is what Ibn al-Jawzee mentioned in his book, *Al-Muntadhim*, on the authority of Muhammad Ibn Moosaa al-Qaadee who said:

"I was present in one of the sittings of Moosaa Ibn Ishaaq al-Qaadee in Rey (a historical city located near Tehran Province, Iran) in 286 A.H. when a woman presented her case. Her gaurdian who was with her claimed that her husband owed her a dowry of 500 dinars that the he refused to pay. al-Qaadee said, 'Do you have your witnesses?' The guardian said, 'I have brought them.' So al-Qadi required that some of the witnesses look at the woman in order to make mention of her in their testimony. One of the witnesses stood up and said to the woman, 'Please stand.' The husband asked, 'What are you going to do?' The witness said, 'We are going to look at your wife while her face is unveiled in order to authenticate our awareness of her.' The husband then said, 'I call upon al-Qaadee to bear witness that she is entitled to this dowry that she claims and her face does not need to be unveiled.' When his wife was informed of what her

---

[45] Imam Ahmad reported it in Musnad Imam Ahmad (2/134, 69,128).

88 | P a g e

husband did, she said, 'Indeed, I call upon al-Qaadee to bear witness that I gifted this dowry to him, and I have absolved him of it in this world and in the Hereafter.' al-Qaadee said, 'This (being jealous for one's wife) should be written down as being from the noble characteristics.'" [46]

Indeed, this should be written down as a noble characteristic, a splendid etiquette and as a lofty value; and where is this from the one who does not stand up for his wife in the least, nor shows these noble values and dignified qualities in front of her at all.

---

[46] In the book, *al-Muntadhim*, by Ibn al-Jawzee (12/403).

ISLĀM LIBERATES THE WOMAN

Indeed, the one who looks at the state of the Muslim woman under the dignified teachings of Islām and tremendous directives will find that Islām liberates her from the claws of depravity and rescues her from the sludge of corruption. She is under the protection and care of Islām in which she lives a life of purity, integrity, praiseworthy concealment and modesty. She is unassailable, exalted under lofty etiquettes, excellent morals and much humility. She is far removed from the nonsense of those preying after women, those who try to defile her, and the snares of criminals. And one who ponders over the woman's circumstance in the pre-Islāmic period of Ignorance and then compares it to her situation in Islām, this reality is plainly evident.

Al-Bukhārī reported in his *Ṣaḥīḥ* on the authority of 'Urwah Ibn az-Zubayr that 'Ā'ishah (رَضِيَاللَّهُعَنْهَا), the wife of the Prophet (صَلَّىاللَّهُعَلَيْهِوَسَلَّمَ), informed him:

أَنَّ النِّكَاحَ فِي الْجَاهِلِيَّةِ كَانَ عَلَى أَرْبَعَةِ أَنْحَاءٍ: فَنِكَاحٌ مِنْهَا نِكَاحُ النَّاسِ الْيَوْمَ، يَخْطُبُ الرَّجُلُ إِلَى الرَّجُلِ وَلِيَّتِهِ أَوْ ابْنَتِهِ فَيُصْدِقُهَا ثُمَّ يَنْكِحُهَا، وَ نِكَاحٌ آخَرُ كَانَ الرَّجُلُ يَقُولُ لِامْرَأَتِهِ إِذَا طَهُرَتْ مِنْ طَمْثِهَا: أَرْسِلِي إِلَى فُلَانٍ فَاسْتَبْضِعِي مِنْهُ ، وَ

يَعْتَزِلُهَا زَوْجُهَا وَ لَا يَمَسُّهَا أَبَداً حَتَّى يَتَبَيَّنَ حَمْلُهَا مِنْ ذَلِكَ الرَّجُلِ الَّذِي تَسْتَبْضِعُ مِنْهُ ، فَإِذَا تَبَيَّنَ حَمْلُهَا أَصَابَهَا زَوْجُهَا إِذَا أَحَبَّ،وَ إِنَّمَا يَفْعَلُ ذَلِكَ رَغْبَةً فِي نَجَابَةِ الْوَلَدِ ، فَكَانَ هَذَا النِّكَاحُ نِكَاحَ الْاسْتِبْضَاعِ ، وَ نِكَاحٌ آخَرُ يَجْتَمِعُ الرَّهْطُ مَا دُونَ الْعَشَرَةِ ، فَيَدْخُلُونَ عَلَى الْمَرْأَةِ كُلُّهُمْ يُصِيبُهَا، فَإِذَا حَمَلَتْ وَ وَضَعَتْ وَ مَرَّ لَيْلٌ بَعْدَ أَنْ تَضَعَ حَمْلَهَا أَرْسَلَتْ إِلَيْهِمْ ، فَلَمْ يَسْتَطِعْ رَجُلٌ مِنْهُمْ أَنْ يَمْتَنِعَ ، حَتَّى يَجْتَمِعُوا عِنْدَهَا تَقُولُ لَهُمْ: قَدْ عَرَفْتُمُ الَّذِي كَانَ مِنْ أَمْرِكُمْ ، وَ قَدْ وَلَدْتُ ، فَهُوَ ابْنُكَ يَا فُلَانُ . تُسَمِّي مَنْ أَحَبَّتْ بِاسْمِهِ ، فَيَلْحَقُ بِهِ وَلَدُهَا،وَ لَا يَسْتَطِيعُ أَنْ يَمْتَنِعَ عَنْهُ الرَّجُلُ ، وَ النِّكَاحُ الرَّابِعُ يَجْتَمِعُ النَّاسُ الْكَثِيرُونَ، فَيَدْخُلُونَ عَلَى الْمَرْأَةِ لَا تَمْنَعُ مَنْ جَاءَهَا وَ هُنَّ الْبَغَايَا ، كُنَّ

يَنْبُضْنَ عَلَى أَبْوَابِهِنَّ الرَّايَاتُ تَكُونُ عَلَماً
، فَمَنْ أَرَادَهُنَّ دَخَلَ عَلَيْهِنَّ ، فَإِذَا حَمَلَتْ
إِحْدَاهُنَّ وَ وَضَعَتْ حَمْلَهَا جَمَعُوا لَهَا وَ
دَعُوا لَهُمُ الْقَافَةَ، ثُمَّ أَلْحَقُوا وَلَدَهَا بِالَّذِي
يَرَوْنَ، فَالْتَاطَتْـهُ بِهِ ، وَ دُعِيَ ابْنُهُ لَا يَمْتَنِعُ
مِنْ ذَلِكَ ، فَلَمَّا بُعِثَ مُحَمَّدٌ صَلَّى اللهُ
عَلَيْهِ وَ سَلَّمَ بِالْحَقِّ هَدَمَ نِكَاحَ الْجَاهِلِيَّةِ
كُلَّهِ إِلَّا نِكَاحَ النَّاسِ الْيَوْمَ.

"That there were four types of marriages during the Pre-Islāmic period of Ignorance. One type was similar to that of the present day: a man would ask the gaurdian of a girl for her hand in marriage, give her *Mahr* and then marry her. The second type was that a man would say to his wife after she had become clean from her period, "Send for so-and-so and have sexual intercourse with him." Her husband would then keep away from her and never sleep with her till she got pregnant from the other man with whom she slept with. When her pregnancy became evident, the husband would sleep with her if he wished. Her husband did so (i.e., let his wife sleep with some other man) so that he might have a child of noble breed. Such a marriage was called as *al-Istibdhaa'*. Another type of marriage was that a group of less than ten men would assemble and enter upon a woman, each would have sexual relation with her. If she became pregnant and delivered a child; after some days had passed, she would send for all of them to come and none of them would refuse. When they all gathered around her, she would say to them, 'You (all) know what you have done, and now I have given birth to a child; So, it is your child o so-and-so,' naming whoever she liked. Her child would then follow that man and he would not refuse to take him. The fourth type of marriage was that many people would enter upon a lady, and she would never reject anyone who came to her; such women were the prostitutes who used to fix flags at their doors as a sign, and he who wished, could have sexual intercourse with them. If any of them got pregnant and delivered a child, then all those men would be gathered for her and they would call the Qafaafah (persons skilled in recognizing the likeness of a child to his father) and would let the child follow the man (whom they saw as his father); and she would let him adhere to him and be called his son with the acceptance of the man. However, when Muhammad (ﷺ) was sent with the Truth, he abolished all the types of marriages observed in the Pre-Islāmic Period of Ignorance except the type of marriage that people recognize today." [47]

Muḥammad Rasheed Ridhaa' also commented in this topic matter by saying:

"the woman would be bought and sold like cattle and goods (commodity). She would be forced into marriage and fornication. She would be inherited, yet not receive an inheritance. She would be someone else's property but could not have possessions. Many of those who own a woman would deny her access to dispose of what belongs to her without their permission. Also, they (the men) viewed that by marriage, they had the right to dispose of her wealth without her permission. In some countries, men differ concerning whether or not the woman is actually a human being that has a soul like the man; whether or not she can learn the religion and if her worship is accepted or not; and also, whether or not she will enter paradise and have a kingdom in the Hereafter.

One of the societies in Rome concluded that the woman is a filthy animal without a soul and an eternal life (in the Hereafter); yet she still must perform acts worship and be at the service of others. Furthermore, they believed that she must

---

[47] al-Bukhārī reported it (5127).

muzzle her mouth like a camel or a voracious dog as to prevent her from laughing, since they viewed her as the trap of Satan. The greatest law amongst them is to allow the father to sell his daughter. Similarly, the Arabs considered that the father also had the right to kill his daughter, rather, even bury her alive. Additionally, some of them viewed that there is no retaliation nor any blood money owed against the man for killing the woman."[48]

And other than these were from the various types of injustices and persecutions that the woman would have to suffer and swallow their bitterness. Women until this present day—not under the shade of Islām—continue to suffer from various types of persecutions, from successive miseries to harsh blows, til some of them wished that they would be treated like the Muslim woman is (in Islām).

The well-known journalist Ms. Annie Rudd[49] said:

"For our girls to work in the homes as servants or like servants is better and lesser of a calamity than for them to be occupied in the factories wherein the girl becomes polluted by the filth that diminishes

---

[48] *Women's rights in Islām* by Muhammad Rasheed Ridhaa' (pg. 6)

[49] Her speech was publicized in the newspaper *Eastern Mill* on May 10, 1901 as it was publicized in the book *Women's rights in Islām* by Muhammad Rasheed Ridhaa' (pg. 76).

the beauty of her life forever. If only our lands were like the lands of the Muslims where there is bashfulness, chastity and purity. The maids and slaves are helped (i.e., with their work) and live in luxury in the most affluent manner. They are also treated in the same fashion as the children (of the house) are treated in which their honor is not violated. Truly, it is a shame on the country of the English for how they made their daughters an example for despicableness due to the prevalent intermixing of the men with them. So what is the matter with us that we do not strive in that which causes the woman to fulfill what agrees with her natural disposition such as staying in the home and abandoning men's occupations designed for men so that she can keep her dignity safe?!"

The English journalist, Lady Cook said in the ECO newspaper:

"Indeed, men have become accustomed to intermingling and because of that the woman aspires for that which contradicts her natural disposition. And the increase in the number of children born out of fornication is according to the increase the intermingling—and this is where the great calamity is for the woman. A man that she would become attached to would leave her (i.e, after having had sexual relations with her) and thus she would suddenly fall into poverty and hardship and taste the bitterness of humiliation and oppression, rather, even death: she is threatened with poverty because pregnancy with its heaviness, cravings and sickness is from the things that prevent a woman from earning an income that she would support herself with; the hardship that she would face is in how she would become a confused scoundrel that does not know what to do with herself; as for the humiliation and disgrace she would face, what could be worse? (i.e., she is already extremely humiliated); and as for her possibly facing death, then this is because many times women [in such a state] commit suicide. And despite all of this, the man is not blamed whatsoever and the woman, instead, has to pay for the consequences even though the causes for such an intermingling that led to this evil result are from the men.

So is not upon us to search for that which would reduce—if not totally remove—these catastrophes that disgrace western civilization?! Should we not adhere to means that would prevent the death of thousands and thousands of innocent children?! The sin is rather on the men who lured the women who, because of their natural inclination to be gentle-hearted, believe their whispers regarding their promises and wishful thinking; and once they satisfied their desires, they leave the women to suffer a painful punishment…"

And like this, women are exposed to varying types of evil, harm and oppression one after the next; and consequently thereafter, suffer the painful punishment and a constricted life and wish to be freed from all of it so that they can live a sound life in agreement with their natural disposition and formation—and so Islām is the only savior for women that can free them from all of those [evils] and actualize for them honor, contentment and tranquility.

ISLĀM PROTECTS THE WOMAN

The religion of Islām has made precise guidelines with which the woman will attain chastity, protection for her private part and safety for her honor. Thus Islām has ordered her to wear the *Hijaab* and awakened her interest in remaining home. Also, it has discouraged her from improperly covering, unveiling her face, leaving the house perfumed and has prevented her from intermingling with the men along with other matters from these great guidelines. The woman has not ordered with all of this except as a means of protecting her from degradation, evil and corruption. It is used to adorn her with chastity and virtue. Islām measures her value to that of a valuable pearl and a precious gem that is guarded against any harm and wickedness.

The following is a summarized look at the most significant of these guidelines and etiquettes for the woman:

The Hijaab:

The woman must conceal her entire body and beauty from foreign men. Allāh (سُبْحَانَهُوَتَعَالَى) says:

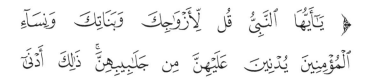

أَن يُعْرَفْنَ فَلَا يُؤْذَيْنَ وَكَانَ ٱللَّهُ غَفُورًا رَّحِيمًا

٥٩

"O Prophet! Tell your wives and your daughters and the women of the believers to draw their cloaks (veils) all over their bodies (i.e., screen themselves completely except the eyes or one eye to see the way). That will be better, that they should be known (as free respectable women) so as not to be annoyed. And Allāh is Ever Oft-Forgiving, Most Merciful." [Sūrah al-ʾAḥzāb (33):59]

And Allāh (سُبْحَانَهُ وَتَعَالَىٰ) says:

وَإِذَا سَأَلْتُمُوهُنَّ مَتَٰعًا فَسْـَٔلُوهُنَّ مِن وَرَآءِ حِجَابٍ ذَٰلِكُمْ أَطْهَرُ لِقُلُوبِكُمْ وَقُلُوبِهِنَّ وَمَا كَانَ لَكُمْ أَن تُؤْذُوا۟ رَسُولَ ٱللَّهِ وَلَآ أَن تَنكِحُوٓا۟ أَزْوَٰجَهُۥ مِنۢ بَعْدِهِۦٓ أَبَدًا إِنَّ ذَٰلِكُمْ كَانَ عِندَ ٱللَّهِ عَظِيمًا

٥٣

"And when you ask (his wives) for anything you want, ask them from behind a screen that is purer for your hearts and their hearts. And it is not (right) for you that you should annoy Allāh's Messenger, nor that you should ever marry his wives after him (his death). Verily! With Allāh, that shall be an enormity." [Sūrah al-'Aḥzāb (33):53]

She should not leave out unless it is for a need:

Allāh (سُبْحَانَهُۥوَتَعَالَىٰٓ) says:

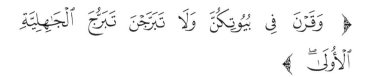

"And stay in your houses, and do not display yourselves like that of the times of ignorance." [Sūrah al-'Aḥzāb (33):33]

And at-Tirmidhī reported in his *Ṣaḥīḥ* that the Prophet (صَلَّىٱللَّهُعَلَيْهِوَسَلَّمَ) said:

الْـمَـرْأَةُ عَـوْرَةٌ ، فَـإِذَا خَـرَجَـتْ اسْـتَـشْـرَفَـهَا الـشَّـيْـطَانُ

"The woman is an *Awrah*[50], so when she goes out, Shaytaan seeks to tempt her." [51]

<u>She should not soften her speech if she is talking with a person for a necessity.</u>

Allāh (سُبْحَانَهُوَتَعَالَى) says:

$$ ﴿ فَلَا تَخْضَعْنَ بِٱلْقَوْلِ فَيَطْمَعَ ٱلَّذِى فِى قَلْبِهِۦ مَرَضٌ وَقُلْنَ قَوْلًا مَّعْرُوفًا ٣٢ ﴾ $$

"Then be not soft in speech, lest he in whose heart is a disease (of hypocrisy, or evil desire for adultery, etc.) should be moved with desire, but speak in an honorable manner." [Sūrah al-'Aḥzāb (33):32]

<u>She should not sit with a non-*Mahram* man in seclusion:</u>

In *Ṣaḥīḥ al-Bukhārī* and *Muslim* on the authority of Ibn 'Abbās (رَضِيَاللَّهُعَنْهُمَا) that the Prophet (صَلَّىاللَّهُعَلَيْهِوَسَلَّمَ) said:

---

[50] **TN:** Ibn Atheer, the author of the book, *an-Nihaayah* (page 649), said about the meaning of this word *Awrah*: "The woman was created as an 'awrah (a concealed part of the body) because whenever she appears, men become shy of her just as they become shy of a private part if exposed.

[51] *Sunan at-Tirmidhi* (#1173).

لَا يَخْلُوَنَّ رَجُلٌ بِامْرَأَةٍ إِلَّا مَعَ ذِي مَحْرِمٍ

"No man should be alone with a lady except in the presence of her *Mahram*." [52]

She should not intermingle with men:

It has been affirmed in the *Ḥadīth* that the Prophet (ﷺ) said:

خَيْرُ صُفُوفِ الـنِّـسَـاءِ آخِرُهَا، وَ شَرُّهَا أَوَّلُـهَا

"The best of the woman's row is the last and the worst of their rows is the first."[53]

This occurs in the masjid, so what is the case in other places. Intermingling has many dangers and harms that have been outlined before.

She should not travel unless a *Mahram* accompanies her:

In *Ṣaḥīḥ Muslim,* on the authority of Abū Hurairah (رضي الله عنه) that the Prophet (ﷺ) said:

---

[52] *Ṣaḥīḥ al-Bukhārī* (#5233) and *Ṣaḥīḥ Muslim* (#1341).

[53] *Ṣaḥīḥ Muslim* (#440).

$$\text{لَا يَـحِـلُّ لِامْـرَأَةٍ أَنْ تُـسَـافِـرَ إِلَّا وَ مَعَـهَا ذُو مَـحْـرِمٍ مِنْـهَا}$$

"It is not lawful for a woman to travel except with a Mahram of her's." [54]

She should not perfume her clothes when going out:

Muslim reported in his *Ṣaḥīḥ* from the Prophet (ﷺ) that he said:

$$\text{إِذَا شَهِـدَتْ إِحْـدَاكُنَّ الْمَـسْـجِـدَ فَـلَا تَمَسَّ طِـيـبـاً}$$

"When one of you women goes to the masjid, she must not put on fragrance." [55]

Al-Imām Ahmad reported from the Prophet (ﷺ) that he said:

---

[54] *Ṣaḥīḥ Muslim* (#1338).

[55] *Ṣaḥīḥ Muslim* (#443).

أَيُّمَا امْرَأَةٍ اسْتَعْطَرَتْ ثُمَّ خَرَجَتْ فَمَرَّتْ عَلَى قَوْمٍ لَيَجِدُوا رِيحَهَا فَهِيَ زَانِيَةٌ، وَ كُلُّ عَيْنٍ زَانِيَةٌ .

"Any woman who perfumes herself and heads out, then passes by some people so that they can smell her fragrance; then she is an adulteress and every eye commits adultery."[56]

She should not attempt to attract the attention of non-Mahram men:

Allāh (سُبْحَانَهُوَتَعَالَى) says:

﴿ وَلَا يَضْرِبْنَ بِأَرْجُلِهِنَّ لِيُعْلَمَ مَا يُخْفِينَ مِن زِينَتِهِنَّ ﴾

"And let them not stamp their feet so as to reveal what they hide of their adornment." [Sūrah an-Nūr (24):31]

She should lower her gaze from looking at non-Mahram men:

---

[56] *Musnad Imam Ahmad* (4/414,418).

Allāh (سُبْحَانَهُوَتَعَالَى) says:

﴿ وَقُل لِّلْمُؤْمِنَٰتِ يَغْضُضْنَ مِنْ أَبْصَٰرِهِنَّ وَيَحْفَظْنَ فُرُوجَهُنَّ ﴾

"And tell the believing women to lower their gaze (from looking at forbidden things), and protect their private parts (from illegal sexual acts, etc.)" [Sūrah an-Nūr (24):31]

She should maintain obedience and worship to her Lord (Allāh):

Allāh (سُبْحَانَهُوَتَعَالَى) says:

﴿ وَأَقِمْنَ ٱلصَّلَوٰةَ وَءَاتِينَ ٱلزَّكَوٰةَ وَأَطِعْنَ ٱللَّهَ وَرَسُولَهُۥٓ إِنَّمَا يُرِيدُ ٱللَّهُ لِيُذْهِبَ عَنكُمُ ٱلرِّجْسَ أَهْلَ ٱلْبَيْتِ وَيُطَهِّرَكُمْ تَطْهِيرًا ۞ ﴾

"And perform *as-Salâh* (*Iqamâtas-Ṣalāh*), and give *Zakâh* and obey Allāh and His Messenger. Allāh wishes only to remove *ar-Rijs* (evil deeds and sins, etc.) from you, O members of the family (of the Prophet), and to purify you with a thorough purification." [Sūrah al-ʾAḥzāb (33):33]

All of these the guidelines as well as others regarding the Muslim woman from what is mentioned in the Qur'ān and the Sunnah are considered to be a safety measure for her and a protector of her honor and dignity. And for this reason, the blessing and bounty of Allāh that He bestowed upon the Muslim woman are tremendously great: He has prepared for her in the religion of Islām causes for happiness, protection of her virtue and chastity, establishment of her dignity, and a repellent for corruption and evil so that she can remain one of a pure soul, taintless character and an unconquerabl state. And to also remain guarded against shamelessness and debasement, as well as what causes deviation, misguidance and decadence.

Indeed, Islām honors the Muslim woman greatly and protects her in the most excellent fashion, as well as guarantee her an honorable life. Her slogan is the veil and chastity. Her garment is purity and integrity. Her banner is the spread of good etiquettes and the establishment of moral character. Her purpose is to protect honor and guard virtue. Thus the Muslim woman will remain strong, of high status and with intact moral character as long as she is adherent to her religion, maintains her Lord's commands, is obedient to her Prophet (ﷺ), submits to Allāh, and complies with His legislation and judgements with complete ease, trust, and tranquility. With this, she will obtain happiness and comfort in this worldly life and will receive great reward and abundant recompense on the Day of Resurrection.

In a Ḥadīth, the Prophet (ﷺ) said:

إِذَا صَلَّتِ الْمَرْأَةُ خَمْسَهَا، وَ صَامَتْ شَهْرَهَا، وَ حَصَنَتْ فَرْجَهَا، وَ أَطَاعَتْ بَعْلَهَا، دَخَلَتْ مِنْ أَيِّ أَبْوَابِ الْجَنَّةِ شَاءَتْ.

"If the woman prays her five prayers, fasts her month (Ramadhaan), protects her private part, and obeys her husband, she will paradise from any gate she wishes."[57]

Al-Imām Ahmad reported the Ḥadīth of ʿAbdur Raḥmān bin ʿAwf (رَضِيَ اللَّهُ عَنْهُ) who said that the Prophet (صَلَّى اللَّهُ عَلَيْهِ وَسَلَّمَ) said:

إِذَا صَلَّتِ الْمَرْأَةُ خَمْسَهَا، وَ صَامَتْ شَهْرَهَا، وَ حَفِظَتْ فَرْجَهَا، وَ أَطَاعَتْ زَوْجَهَا قِيلَ لَهَا : ادْخُلِي الْجَنَّةَ مِنْ أَيِّ أَبْوَابِ الْجَنَّةِ شِئَتْ.

"If the woman prays her five prayers, fasts her month (Ramadhaan), preserves her private part,

---

[57] Ṣaḥīḥ Ibn Hibbaan (#4163).

and obeys her husband, it will be said to her, 'Enter paradise from any gate you wish.'" [58]

So congratulations to the Muslim woman for this honorable promise and great virtue granted to her as long as she lives her life adhering to this noble directive disregarding the heedlessness of the people from those who call to wickedness and trials:

$$﴿ وَٱللَّهُ يُرِيدُ أَن يَتُوبَ عَلَيْكُمْ وَيُرِيدُ ٱلَّذِينَ يَتَّبِعُونَ ٱلشَّهَوَٰتِ أَن تَمِيلُواْ مَيْلًا عَظِيمًا ٢٧ ﴾$$

"Allāh wishes to accept your repentance, but those who follow their lusts, wish that you (believers) should deviate tremendously away from the Right Path." [Sūrah An-Nisā' (4):27]

It is truly distressing to see the malicious assaults, spiteful conspiracies and criminalistics plans that the Muslim woman is exposed to in these current times; all leading to the destruction of her decency, ripping apart her honor, demolishing her dignity, and burying her moral excellence, religion and faith and thus connecting her to whores and immoral women. And all of this is through the destructive satellite channels, wasteful obscene magazines, her busying herself with all types of see-through, provocative clothing

---

[58] *Musnad Ahmad* (1/191).

and her heart inciting her to love imitating the non-Muslim women who walk the earth without any faith, morals or etiquettes that would restrain them. Also, through her being dragged to abandon the legislation of Islām through her running after all of that, being dragged to wickedness and being distanced from the sources of decency, moral excellence—may Allāh make it impossible for them to fulfill their wishes [to ruin the Muslim woman].

ESSENTIAL CLARIFICATIONS

In a time when some sick individuals and the masters of desires rejoice—from those who do not care for the legislative guidelines and established boundaries that actualize the woman's dignity, and guarantee her might and happiness—and advocate for her so-called rights and hysterical liberties; the woman is dragged to outcomes whose end-consequences cannot be imaged and abysses whose evil and danger are unknown all under shining banners and captivating slogans: they take advantage of and overcome the woman's affections, hastiness in reacting, and her deficiency in considering the end-consequences of matters.

In this era the statements from the sincere, advising people of knowledge, truthful callers and propagative jealous individuals work to restrain the women from falling into these abysses and regressing in these evil paths as to preserve her dignity and honor. Also to preserve her flank and excellent behavior, keeping it from being polluted with the filth of corruption.

Surely, amongst the greatest benefits that the woman should acquaint herself with in this subject is the clarification that was issued on these topics by the Permanent Committee for Scholastic Research and Religious Verdicts on the 25th of

Muharram[59] in the year 1420 A.H. (which corresponds with May 6, 1999) and the text is as follows:

"All praise and thanks belong to Allāh alone and May He send His *Salaah* and *Salaam* upon His Messenger, family and companions as well as whomever is led by his guidance:

To proceed:

Among the matters which are unhidden from every Muslim who has insight of his religion is what the Muslim woman experiences under the shade of Islām—specifically in this country (i.e., Saudi Arabia)—of dignity, bashfulness, appropriate work for her, acquisition of her legislative rights which Allāh has made obligatory for her (to receive) contrary to how a woman lived in the pre-Islāmic era of ignorance and continues to live today in some societies that contradict Islām's etiquettes in their neglect, wastefulness and oppression.

This is a blessing we should thank Allāh for and are obliged to maintain. However, there are groups of people whose cultivation has been contaminated by western views that are displeased with this honorable reality that the woman enjoys in our country from modesty, covering and protection. They want the Muslim woman to resemble the women in the lands of the disbelievers and secularists; thus they have started

---

[59] **Translator's notes:** *Muharam* is the first month in the Islāmic calendar.

writing in newspapers and demanding things in the name of women matters that are summarized in the following:

The first matter: Ripping apart the *Hijaab* which Allāh has commanded in His statement:

﴿ يَٰٓأَيُّهَا ٱلنَّبِىُّ قُل لِّأَزْوَٰجِكَ وَبَنَاتِكَ وَنِسَآءِ ٱلْمُؤْمِنِينَ يُدْنِينَ عَلَيْهِنَّ مِن جَلَٰبِيبِهِنَّ ذَٰلِكَ أَدْنَىٰٓ أَن يُعْرَفْنَ فَلَا يُؤْذَيْنَ ﴾

"**O Prophet! Tell your wives and your daughters and the women of the believers to draw their cloaks (veils) all over their bodies (i.e., screen themselves completely except the eyes or one eye to see the way). That will be better, that they should be known (as free respectable women) so as not to be annoyed.**" [Sūrah al-ʾAḥzāb (33):59]

And with His statement:

﴿ وَإِذَا سَأَلْتُمُوهُنَّ مَتَٰعًا فَسْـَٔلُوهُنَّ مِن وَرَآءِ حِجَابٍ ذَٰلِكُمْ أَطْهَرُ لِقُلُوبِكُمْ وَقُلُوبِهِنَّ ﴾

"**And when you ask (his wives) for anything you want, ask them from behind a screen that is purer for your hearts and for their hearts.**" [Sūrah al-ʾAḥzāb (33):53]

And with His statement:

$$\{ \text{وَلْيَضْرِبْنَ بِخُمُرِهِنَّ عَلَى جُيُوبِهِنَّ} \}$$

"And to draw their veils all over Juyubihinna (i.e., their bodies, faces, necks and bosoms, etc.)." [Sūrah an-Nūr (24):31]

And the statement of ʿĀʾishah (رَضِيَاللَّهُعَنْهَا) in the story about when she fell behind from the caravan and Sufyān ibn Muʾattil (رَضِيَاللَّهُعَنْهُ) passed by her and how she placed her *Kkhimaar* over her face when she saw him. She said:

$$\text{وَقَدْ رَآنِي قَبْلَ الْـحِجَابِ}$$

"And he recognized me on seeing me as he had seen me before the order of compulsory veiling (was prescribed)."

And her statement:

$$\text{كُنَّا مَعَ النَّبِيِّ (صَلَّى اللهُ عَلَيْهِ وَسَلَّمَ) وَنَـحْنُ مُـحْرِمَاتٌ فَإِذَا}$$
$$\text{مَرَّ بِنَا الرَّجُلُ سَدَلَتْ إِحْدَانَا خِمَارَهَا عَلَى وَجْهِهَا، فَإِذَا جَاوَزُونَا}$$
$$\text{كَشَفْنَاهُ.}$$

"We were with the Prophet (صَلَّىاللَّهُعَلَيْهِوَسَلَّمَ), and we were in *Ihraam*. When men met us, we would lower our garments from the top of our heads, and when they had gone, we would lift them up again."

And so forth from what attests to the obligation of the Muslim woman wearing the Hijab from the Qur'ān and the Sunnah. These individuals desire from the woman that she contradicts the Book of her Lord and Sunnah of her Prophet and thus becomes unveiled so that every eager person and anyone with a disease within in his heart could take pleasure in looking at her.

The second matter: They demand that women should be allowed to drive cars in spite of what results from that of corruption and her exposure to dangers which are not hidden from the insightful person.

The third matter: They demand to take pictures of women and place them on cards exclusive to them that are circulated; and consequently, anyone who has a sickness in his heart aspires her. And without a doubt this a means that leads to the removal of the *Hijaab*.

The fourth matter: They also demand the intermingling of women with men and that she assume jobs which are specifically for men and abandon her appropriate job (role) which is harmonious to her natural disposition and modesty. They allege that restricting her to her suitable role (work) is a hindrance to her; there is no doubt that this contradicts reality. Surely, what is a hindrance to her in reality is her appointment to jobs that are inappropriate for her—a matter that goes against what the legislation mentions regarding its prevention of the mixing between the two sexes, the woman being alone with a man with whom it is impermissible for her to be alone, as well as her traveling without a *Mahram* due to what results from these matters of dangerous harms that lead to a dispraised end.

The religion of Islām prevents intermingling of men and women even in places of worship. Their place in the prayer has been made to be behind the men and she is actually encouraged to pray in her home as the Prophet (ﷺ) said:

$$\text{لَا تَمْنَعُوا إِمَاءَ اللهِ مَسَاجِدَ اللهِ وَبُيُوتُهُنَّ خَيْرٌ لَهُنَّ}$$

"Do not prevent your women from visiting the mosque; but their houses are better for them (for praying)."

All of this is for the purpose of safeguarding the woman's dignity and keeping her distant from the things that cause *Fitnah*. Therefore, Muslims are obliged to preserve the dignity of their women and not look at these misleading propagandas. They should take a warning from what has befallen women in the societies where these propagandas are accepted and women are deceived by them resulting in evil consequences. The happy person is the one who takes an admonition from others.

The Muslim rulers in these countries are obliged to seize the hands of the foolish and prevent them from disseminating their evil views in order to protect the society from its evil effects and disastrous consequences. The Prophet (ﷺ) said:

$$\text{مَا تَرَكْتُ بَعْدِي فِتْنَةً أَضَرَّ عَلَى الرِّجَالِ مِنَ النِّسَاءِ}$$

"I have not left a more harmful fitnah upon the men than women."

And He (ﷺ) said:

وَاسْتَوْصُوا بِالنِّسَاءِ

"Treat the woman well."

And preserving their dignity and chastity as well as keeping them distant from things that cause *Fitnah* is from treating them well.

May Allāh grant all of us success towards the good and righteousness and May He send His *Salaah* and *Salaam* upon our Prophet, his family and companions."

Then the signatures of the members of the committee were added and they are:

* ❖ His eminence Shaykh ʿAbdul ʿAzīz bin Bāz (رَحِمَهُ ٱللَّهُ),
* ❖ His eminence Shaykh ʿAbdul ʿAzīz Aal Shaykh,
* ❖ Shaykh ʿAbdullāh al-Ghudayyaan (رَحِمَهُ ٱللَّهُ),
* ❖ Shaykh Abū Zayd and Shaykh Ṣāliḥ al-Fawzān.

May Allāh be good to them and reward them with the best reward. May He cause others to benefit by their diligent efforts and place blessings in their deeds.

The date in which this clarification originated was on the 25th of *Muharram* in 1420 A.H. just two days before the passing away of the his eminence Shaykh Ibn Bāz. This is to attest to the greatness of his advices and complete instructions up until the last days of his life (رَحِمَهُ ٱللَّه)—and this was a farewell advice from this sincere Imam. May Allāh give him the best reward for aiding the Muslims and make his final abode in *al-Firdows* (i.e., the highest station in paradise).

The issue of the woman placing the 'Abā'ah on the shoulders and its legislative description for the woman

Likewise among the religious verdicts issued by the Permanent Committee for Scholastic Research and Religious verdicts on this matter which is appropriate for the sincere Muslim woman to ponder over and take benefit from is the following. And this verdict was issued by the standing committee on the 9th of *Rabee' Awwal* in 1421 A.H. about the issue of the woman placing the *'Abā'ah* (the loose outer garment usually worn under the Jilbaab) on the shoulders and its legislative description for the woman. The following is what was said:

"All praise and thanks belong to Allāh alone and may He send His *Salaah* and *Salaam* upon the one whom will not be preceded by any other prophet.

To proceed:

After the Standing Committee for Scholastic Research and Verdicts looked over what was mentioned to His eminence, the Mufti (i.e., Shaykh ʿAbdul-ʿAzīz bin Muhammad Aal Shaykh) from the individual that was seeking a verdict, the question was transferred to the Committee of General Safety for the Body of Senior Scholars (#934) on the 12th of Safar in 1421 A.H. The questioner asked:

'Lately, an *'Abā'ah* that shows the shape of the body and is tight has been circulating; it consists of two thin layers made of crepe fabric, two long sleeves, embroidery and is placed on the shoulders. So what is the religious ruling concerning this type of *'Abā'ah*? Please give us a *Fataawa*, may you be rewarded with good; also we wish that it be addressed to the Ministry of Commerce in order to prevent this type of *'Abā'ah* and its likes.'

After the committee discussed this request for a religious verdict, they responded that the legislative *'Abā'ah* for the woman is the *Jilbaab* that establishes what is intended in the Qur'ān and Sunnah completely covering the body and being distancing [the women] from *Fitnah*. And in light of this, the Muslim woman's *'Abā'ah* must meet the following requirements:

The first requirement: It must be thick, not revealing what is underneath and cannot be close fitted.

The second requirement: It must cover the whole body and be loose fitted, not revealing its shape.

The third requirement: It must only open in the front and the holes for the sleeves are restricted.

The fourth requirement: It must not have on it any adornments that will direct glances at her or it. It is imperative that is devoid of any symbols, ornaments, writings, or signs.

The fifth reuqirement: It must not resemble the clothing of the disbelieving women or men.

The sixth requirement: The *'Abā'ah* must be placed over the head initially.

According to what has been previously mentioned, the *'Abā'ah* cited in the question is not a legitimate one for the Muslim woman; and it is not permissible for her to wear it due to the fact that the legislative requirements are not met. Also, it is impermissible to import such an *'Abā'ah*, manufacture it, sell it or disseminate it amongst the Muslims; because doing so is deemed cooperating upon sin and transgression. Allāh (جَلَّ وَعَلَا) says:

$$﴿ وَتَعَاوَنُوا۟ عَلَى ٱلْبِرِّ وَٱلتَّقْوَىٰ وَلَا تَعَاوَنُوا۟ عَلَى ٱلْإِثْمِ وَٱلْعُدْوَٰنِ ۚ وَٱتَّقُوا۟ ٱللَّهَ ۖ إِنَّ ٱللَّهَ شَدِيدُ ٱلْعِقَابِ ٢ ﴾$$

'Help you one another in *al-Birr* and *at-Taqwā* (virtue, righteousness and piety); but do not help one another in sin and transgression. And fear Allāh. Verily, Allāh is Severe in punishment.'
[Sūrah Al-Mā'idah (5):2]

And when the Committee has clarified this as an advice to the believing women to have *Taqwā* of Allāh (i.e., to obey the commands & stay away from the prohibitions), abide to completely covering the body from foreign men with the *Jilbaab* and *khimar*, it is out of obedience to Allāh (سُبْحَانَهُ وَتَعَالَى) and His Messenger (صَلَّى ٱللَّهُ عَلَيْهِ وَسَلَّمَ) and distancing from things that bring about *Fitnah*—and with Allāh alone is *Tawfiiq*. May He send His *Salaah* and *Salaam* upon our Prophet Muhammad, his family and companions."

Then the signatures of the members of the committee were added and they are:

- ❖ Shaykh ʿAbdul-ʿAzīz Ibn ʿAbdullāh bin Muḥammad Aal Shaykh,
- ❖ Shaykh ʿAbdullāh bin ʿAbdur-Raḥmān al-Ghudayyān,
- ❖ Shaykh Ṣāliḥ bin Fawzān al-Fawzān,
- ❖ and Shaykh Bakr Ibn ''Abdullah Abū Zayd.

How the Woman Should Dress Around her Mahaarim

Another clarification was issued by the Committee on the 25ᵗʰ of *Muharram* in 1421 concerning the woman's dress around her *Mahaarim* (plural for *Mahram*) and other women.

The following is what was said:

"All praise and thanks belong to Allāh, the Lord of all that exists; and May Allāh send His *Salaah* and *Salaam* upon our Prophet Muhammad, his family and all of his companions.

To proceed:

The believing woman in the beginning of Islām had reached the utmost degree of purity, chastity, modesty and decency by the grace of believing in Allāh and His Messenger and adhering to the Qur'ān and Sunnah. The women in that era wore clothes that concealed what was underneath; and revealing themselves or displaying common, vulgar manners was not known from them in their gatherings with one another or with their *Mahaarim*. And this upright Sunnah has come to pass as being from the actions of the women of this Ummah—and all praise belongs to Allāh—generation after generation until this recent era. Then corruption in woman's clothing and morals had crept into many Muslim women from many avenues—and this is a matter that is not simple.

After examining many requests for legal rulings (i.e., *Fatāwā*) presented to the Permanent Committee for Scholastic Research and Religious Verdicts regarding the restrictions for a woman looking at another and what is binding upon them to wear around each other, the committee explained to the Muslim women in general that they should mold themselves with modesty—a manner that Prophet (ﷺ) made to be from true faith and one of its branches. And from the modesty that we are commanded with legislatively as well as customarily, is that the Muslim woman covering herself, being bashful and molding herself with morals that distance her from situations that bring about *Fitnah* and doubt.

The apparentness of the Qur'ān attests to the fact that the Muslim woman should not display to another woman anything except that which she displays to her *Mahaarim* from what is customarily shown in the house and at work just as Allāh (ﷻ) says:

﴿ وَلَا يُبْدِينَ زِينَتَهُنَّ إِلَّا مَا ظَهَرَ مِنْهَا وَلْيَضْرِبْنَ بِخُمُرِهِنَّ عَلَىٰ جُيُوبِهِنَّ وَلَا يُبْدِينَ زِينَتَهُنَّ إِلَّا لِبُعُولَتِهِنَّ أَوْ ءَابَاۤئِهِنَّ أَوْ ءَابَاۤءِ بُعُولَتِهِنَّ أَوْ أَبْنَاۤئِهِنَّ أَوْ أَبْنَاۤءِ بُعُولَتِهِنَّ أَوْ إِخْوَٰنِهِنَّ أَوْ بَنِىٓ إِخْوَٰنِهِنَّ أَوْ بَنِىٓ أَخَوَٰتِهِنَّ أَوْ نِسَاۤئِهِنَّ ﴾

"And not to reveal their adornment except to their husbands, their fathers, their husband's fathers, their sons, their husband's sons, their brothers or

their brother's sons, or their sister's sons, or their (Muslim) women (i.e., their sisters in Islām)." [Sūrah an-Nūr (24):31]

Since this is a text from the Qur'ān and that which the Sunnah attests to, it was also the custom of the Messenger's wives—the female companions—as well as those who followed them in excellence from the women of this Ummah until our recent times. And what has become common practice to uncover is cited in the noble verse: that which mostly becomes apparent in the house and when laboring and is difficult to constantly safeguard such as the uncovering of the head, hands, neck and feet. As for a woman exaggerating in uncovering herself, then there is not a single evidence from the Qur'ān or Sunnah attesting to its permissibility; in addition, it is a matter that causes the woman to be tried by *Fitnah* and tempt other women from her gender—and this is something present amongst them. Also, such an action (the woman extravagantly uncovering herself) is a bad example for other women in what lies in it of resembling the disbelieving women, prostitutes and shameless women in their dress. It has been authentically reported from the Prophet (صَلَّى ٱللَّهُ عَلَيْهِ وَسَلَّمَ) that he said:

مَنْ تَشَبَّهَ بِقَوْمٍ فَهُوَ مِنْهُمْ

'Whoever imitates a people is from them.'

Al-Imām Ahmad and Abū Daawood reported it. Also, in *Sahīh Muslim* on the authority of "'Abdullāh Ibn 'Umar who said that the Prophet (ﷺ) saw on him two pieces of dyed clothing and then said:

إِنَّ هَذِهِ مِنْ ثِيَابِ الْكُفَّارِ فَلَا تَلْسَبْهَا

'Indeed this is from the clothing of the disbeliever, so do not wear it.'

And in *Ṣaḥīḥ Muslim* the Prophet (ﷺ) said:

صِنْفَانِ مِنْ أَهْلِ النَّارِ لَمْ أَرَهُمَا قَوْمٌ مَعَهُمْ سِيَاطٌ كَأَذْنَابِ الْبَقَرِ يَضْرِبُونَ بِهَا النَّاسَ وَنِسَاءٌ كَاسِيَاتٌ عَارِيَاتٌ مُمِيلاَتٌ مَائِلاَتٌ رُءُوسُهُنَّ كَأَسْنِمَةِ الْبُخْتِ الْمَائِلَةِ لاَ يَدْخُلْنَ الْجَنَّةَ وَلاَ يَجِدْنَ رِيحَهَا وَإِنَّ رِيحَهَا لَيُوجَدُ مِنْ مَسِيرَةِ كَذَا وَكَذَا

"There are two types of people of the Hell fire that I have seen: one of them is a people that possess whips like the tails of a cow and flog people with it, the second one is women who would be naked in spite of their being dressed, who are seduced (to wrong paths) and seduce others with their hair high like humps. These women will not enter Paradise and they would not find the scent of Paradise even though its fragrance can be found from such and such distance (from a great distance)."

And the meaning of **"Women who would be naked in spite of their being dressed,"** is the woman who dresses with clothes that do not conceal her and she is in reality naked. She is like the one who wears thin clothes that show her skin, or tight ones that show the shape of her body, or short clothing that does not cover some parts of her body.

Therefore, what is obligatory upon the believing women is to be committed to the guidance of the mothers of the believers, the female companions and those women of this Ummah who followed them in excellence; and aspire to remain veiled and have modesty as that keeps the woman distant from things that bring about *Fitnah* and it is a form of protection for the soul from things that propagate lowly desires and falling into lewdness.

And Just as the Muslim women are commanded to be cautious from falling into what Allāh and His Messenger have made unlawful from the wearing of clothing that resembles the disbelieving women and prostitutes out of obedience to Allāh and His Messenger and hoping for Allāh's reward and fearing His chastisement; it is incumbent upon every Muslim man to fear Allāh regarding those whom are under his care from the women.

Thus, he must not leave them to wear what Allāh and His Messenger have made unlawful from the bawdy, revealing and seductive clothes. Also, he must know that he is a guardian over his flock and will be questioned [about them] on the Day of Resurrection.

We ask Allāh to rectify the Muslims' circumstances and guide us all to the straight path—indeed, Allāh is All-Hearing, near and answers the supplicant. And may He send

Salaah and *Salaam* upon our Prophet Muhammad, his family and companions."

Then the signatures of the members of the committee were added and they are:

- ❖ Shaykh ʿAbdul-ʿAzīz bin ʿAbdullāh bin Muḥammad Aal Shaykh,
- ❖ Shaykh ʿAbdullāh bin ʿAbdur Raḥmān al-Ghudayyaan,
- ❖ Shaykh Ṣāliḥ bin Fawzān al-Fawzān,
- ❖ and Shaykh Bakr Ibn ʿAbdullāh Abū Zayd.

The Committee's Clarification Concerning Lewd Magazines and Their Dangers

All praise belongs to Allāh alone and may He send *Ṣalāh* and *Salaam* upon our Prophet Muhammad, his family, and companions.

To proceed:

In this era, the Muslims are stricken by great trials and temptations that close in on them from all sides; and consequently, many of them fall into these temptations. These evil deeds have become apparent and the people have come to disclose them without any fear or shyness, and the reason for this is due to their indifference to Allaah's religion, lack of concern for its guidelines and legislation and the heedlessness of many of the reformers on how to establish Allaah's legislation and command the good and prohibit the evil. There is no deliverance or salvation for the Muslims from these calamities and temptations except through sincere repentance to Allāh (سُبْحَانَهُوَتَعَالَ), giving great importance to His commands and prohibitions, and stopping the foolish and ordering them with the truth.

Indeed, from the greatest temptations which have surfaced in our era is the action of those who deal in corruption, the middlemen of wickedness, those who love to spread lewdness amongst the believers through their publishing of wicked magazines that oppose the commands and prohibitions of Allāh and His Messenger. Throughout their pages, there are various types of revealing pictures and faces that tempt and incite the desires as well as bring about corruption.

Through thorough investigations, it has been affirmed that these magazines use numerous tactics to propagate immorality, wickedness and the enfluence one's wimps and desires towards what Allāh and His Messenger have made unlawful.

These types of magazines include the following:

Firstly: Seductive pictures on the cover and inside of the magazines.

Secondly: Women in full beauty inciting temptation and deceiving others with it.

Thirdly: Vile and shameless statements as well as poetic and prose writing that are far from modesty and nobility, destroy morals and corrupt the *Ummah* (the Muslim nation).

Forthly: Stories of disgraceful romances and reports of male and female actors and dancers from the open sinners.

Fifthly: A clear call to women to improperly adorn themselves, show their faces, the intermingling of the sexes and the tearing of the *Hijaab*.

Sixthly: The display of tempting and revealing clothing to the believing women in order to deceive them into becoming nude, undressing and imitating prostitutes and wicked women.

Seventhly: Are hugging, embracing, and kissing between men and women.

Eightly: Within these magazines are blazing articles that excite the lifeless sexual urges inside the male and female youth; thus it forcefully thrusts them into taking a path of temptations and misguidance, and falling into indecency, sinning, lustful love and passion. How many male and female youngsters have fallen into violent passions due to these poisonous magazines?! And because of them, they fell into destruction and crossed the boundaries of their natural disposition and religion. Indeed, these magazines have changed the thinking of many people regarding the rulings of the *Sharee'ah* (Islāmic Legislation) and the fundamental principles of the sound natural disposition due their propagation of articles and mere posed-opinions. Hence many of the people have to come to enjoy sinning, wickedness and transgressing the boundaries of Allaah due to reliance on these magazines and their domination over the peoples' intellects and thoughts.

So basically, the main objective of these magazines is to make business with the woman's body which is aided by Satan with all the possible causes of deception and means of *Fitnah* in order to spread pornography, the shaming of women, the corrupting of the believing women specifically and the changing of Muslim communities to flocks of animals: flocks that know neither good nor detest evil, nor give any weight or care to the application of Allaah's purifying legislation as is the case with many communities; rather, in some of them, the matter has reached to the point where the two sexes enjoy each other completely nude in what is called, "The Cities of the Nude," and refuge is sought with Allaah from the relapsing of the natural disposition and falling into what Allaah and His Messenger have prohibited.

And this on the grounds of what was already mentioned regarding the reality of these magazines, what is known from its evil goals and effects, as well as the many complaints that are reported to the Committee by those extremely jealous [for the Muslim woman] from the scholars, students of knowledge and the general Muslims regarding the spreading of these magazines' exhibition in bookstores, convenient stores and business markets. Thus the Permanent Committee for Scholastic Research and Religious Verdicts has concluded the following:

First: It is impermissible to publish the likes of these lowly magazines whether they are general or specific for women's clothing; and whoever does this will have his share from Allāh's (سُبْحَانَهُوَتَعَالَى) statement:

إِنَّ ٱلَّذِينَ يُحِبُّونَ أَن تَشِيعَ ٱلْفَٰحِشَةُ فِي ٱلَّذِينَ ءَامَنُواْ لَهُمْ عَذَابٌ أَلِيمٌ فِي ٱلدُّنْيَا وَٱلْأَخِرَةِ وَٱللَّهُ يَعْلَمُ وَأَنتُمْ لَا تَعْلَمُونَ ﴿١٩﴾

"**Verily, those who like that (the crime of) illegal sexual intercourse should be propagated among those who believe, they will have a painful torment** in this world and in the Hereafter." [Sūrah an-Nūr (24):19]

Second: It is impermissible to work with these magazines in any way, regardless whether the work is in its management, release, printing or distribution; because that would be assisting in disobedience, falsehood and corruption and Allāh (﷾) says:

﴿ وَلَا تَعَاوَنُوا۟ عَلَى ٱلْإِثْمِ وَٱلْعُدْوَٰنِ وَٱتَّقُوا۟ ٱللَّهَ إِنَّ ٱللَّهَ شَدِيدُ ٱلْعِقَابِ ۝ ﴾

"But do not help one another in sin and transgression. And fear Allāh. Verily, Allāh is Severe in punishment." [Sūrah Al-Māʾidah (5):2]

Third: It is impermissible to advertise for and promote these magazines as this is a form of directing and calling to evil. It has been affirmed from the Prophet (ﷺ) that he said:

وَمَنْ دَعَا إِلَى ضَلَالَةٍ كَانَ عَلَيْهِ مِنَ الْإِثْمِ مِثْلَ آثَامِ مَنْ تَبِعَهُ لَا يَنْقُصُ ذَلِكَ مِنْ آثَامِهِمْ شَيْئًا.

"And whoever invites others to follow a misguidance will incur a sin equivalent to that of

the one who followed him (in sinfulness) without their sins being diminished in any respect.'[60]

Fourth: It is impermissible to sell these magazines, and the earned income from it is an impermissible one. And it is compulsory upon whoever falls into anything from that to repent to Allāh (سُبْحَانَهُوَتَعَالَى) and free himself from this filthy earning.

Fifth: It is impermissible for the Muslim to purchase and acquire these magazines due to the trials and evils that they contain; and also because purchasing them increases the income and monetary funds of its owners, and encourages them to produce and promote more. It is likewise upon the Muslim to be cautious of his family (whether male or female) becoming attached to these magazines so as to protect them from their *Fitnah* and enchantment. Hence the Muslim must know that he is a shepherd and responsible for his flock on the Day of Judgement.

Sixth: It is upon the Muslim to lower his gaze from looking at these corrupt magazines out of obedience to Allaah and His Messenger (صَلَّأَللَّهُعَلَيْهِوَسَلَّمَ) and as a means to distance himself from *Fitnah* and its places. Similarly, it is upon the Muslim to not claim safety for himself; for indeed, the Prophet (صَلَّأَللَّهُعَلَيْهِوَسَلَّمَ) has informed us that Satan flows in man

---

[60] Reported by Muslim

like blood (i.e., man is not safe from his temptations). And al-Imām Ahmad (ﷺ) said:

'How many a gaze has cast into the heart of the one looking a calamity.'

So whoever becomes attached to these magazines for their pictures and the likes, it will ruin his heart and life and busy him with that which will not benefit him in his Worldly-life and Hereafter. This is because the rectification of the heart and its life is only possible through attachment to Allaah (جَلَّ جَلَالُهُ), His worship and secret discourse with Him; as well as through sincerity for Him and being filled with His love (سُبْحَانَهُ وَتَعَالَى).

Seventh: It is an obligation upon whomever Allāh has given rule to over any of the Muslim lands to advise the Muslims, protect them from corruption and its people, and distance them from all that which will harm them in their religion and Worldly-life. From this, is preventing the spreading and distribution of these corruptive magazines and restraining their evil from them; and this is a type of aiding Allāh and his religion and is from the causes of success, salvation and establishment in the earth as Allāh (سُبْحَانَهُ وَتَعَالَى) has said:

﴿ ٱلَّذِينَ أُخْرِجُوا۟ مِن دِيَٰرِهِم بِغَيْرِ حَقٍّ إِلَّآ أَن يَقُولُوا۟ رَبُّنَا ٱللَّهُ وَلَوْلَا دَفْعُ ٱللَّهِ ٱلنَّاسَ بَعْضَهُم بِبَعْضٍ لَّهُدِّمَتْ صَوَٰمِعُ وَبِيَعٌ وَصَلَوَٰتٌ وَمَسَٰجِدُ يُذْكَرُ فِيهَا ٱسْمُ ٱللَّهِ ﴾

كَثِيرًا وَلَيَنصُرَنَّ ٱللَّهُ مَن يَنصُرُهُۥٓ إِنَّ ٱللَّهَ لَقَوِيٌّ
عَزِيزٌ ۝ ٱلَّذِينَ إِن مَّكَّنَّٰهُمْ فِى ٱلْأَرْضِ أَقَامُوا۟ ٱلصَّلَوٰةَ
وَءَاتَوُا۟ ٱلزَّكَوٰةَ وَأَمَرُوا۟ بِٱلْمَعْرُوفِ وَنَهَوْا۟ عَنِ ٱلْمُنكَرِ
وَلِلَّهِ عَٰقِبَةُ ٱلْأُمُورِ ۝

"Verily, Allāh will help those who help His (Cause).
Truly, Allāh is All-Strong, All-Mighty. (40) Those
(Muslim rulers) who, if We give them power in the
land, (they) enjoin Iqamat-as-Ṣalāh. [i.e. to
perform the five compulsory congregational Ṣalāh
(prayers) (the males in mosques)], to pay the Zakâh
and they enjoin al-Ma'rûf (i.e., Islāmic
Monotheism and all that Islām orders one to do),
and forbid al-Munkar (i.e. disbelief, polytheism
and all that Islām has forbidden) [i.e. they make the
Qur'ān as the law of their country in all the spheres
of life]. And with Allāh rests the end of (all) matters
(of creatures)." [Sūrah al-Ḥajj (22):40-41]

And all praise and thanks are for the Lord of the universe
and may His *Ṣalāh* and *Salaam* be upon our Prophet
Muhammad, his family, companions and whoever followed
them in goodness until the Day of Recompense. With Allāh
is success and may he raise the rank of our Prophet
Muhammad and grant him, his family and companions
peace."

Then it was concluded with the signatures of the Committee members and they are:

- ❖ His Eminence Shaykh ʿAbdul- ʿAzīz bin ʿʿAbdullāh Ibn Muhammad Aal Shaykh,
- ❖ his eminence Shaykh ʿʿAbdullāh Ibn ʿAbdur-Rahmaan al-Ghudayyaan,
- ❖ his eminence Shaykh Saalih Ibn Fawzaan al-Fawzān,
- ❖ and his eminence Shaykh Bakr Abū Zayd.

And with this we will conclude this treatise. We ask Allaah to reform the Muslim girls and women and that he protect them from the *Fitan,* that which is apparent from it and that which is hidden. And the close of our request will be: All praise and thanks are for Allaah, the lord of all that exists and may He send *Salaah* and *Salaam* upon our Prophet Muhammad and the whole of his family and companions.

Made in the USA
Columbia, SC
30 April 2024

34829111R00083